EXPLORING THE CHESAPEAKE
IN SMALL BOATS

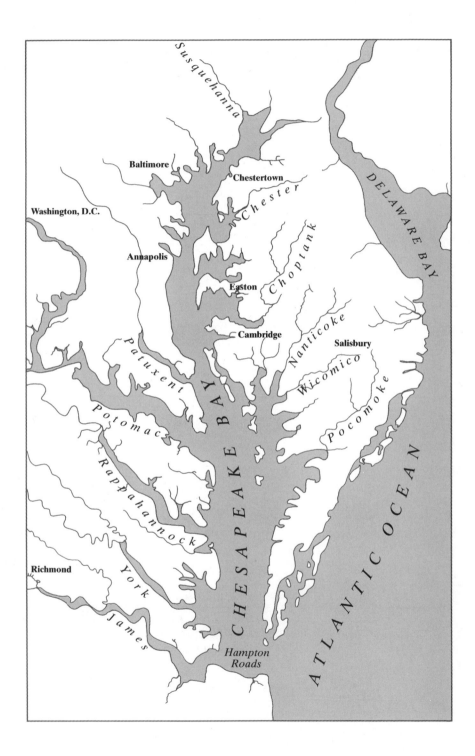

EXPLORING THE CHESAPEAKE IN SMALL BOATS

By

John Page Williams, Jr.

Photographs By William S. Portlock

Tidewater Publishers
Centreville, Maryland

Cover photos by William S. Portlock and Dan Bellinger.

Library of Congress Cataloging-in-Publication Data

Williams,   John Page
    Exploring the Chesapeake in small boats / by John Page Williams,
Jr. ; photographs by William S. Portlock. — 1st ed.
        p.   cm.
    Includes index.
    ISBN 0-87033-429-8 (pbk.)   :
    1. Natural history—Chesapeake Bay (Md. and Va.)   2. Boats and
boating—Chesapeake Bay (Md. and Va.)   3. Chesapeake Bay (Md. and
Va.)—Guidebooks.   I. Title.
QH104.5.C45W48   1992
508.3163'47—dc20   91-50582
                                                              CIP

Manufactured in the United States of America
First edition, 1992; fourth printing, 2000

Contents

Part Two: Trip Suggestions

Foreword

In nearly twenty years of reporting and writing on the Chesapeake Bay, there were perhaps a few dozen days' experiences that gave me more insight and enthusiasm for the Bay and the region than all the other days combined. Sometimes the experience was reading a particularly fine evocation of nature or place, or attending a superbly organized conference on the issues. But more often than not these golden moments and quantum leaps involved days afield or afloat with those rare individuals who combine intimate knowledge and love of nature with a powerful ability to communicate it.

One of them is John Page Williams, this book's author and a master educator. Singlehanded, and probably with the thought that someday he would have to grow up and get a real job, he began running field trips for the fledgling Chesapeake Bay Foundation nearly two decades ago. With the foundation now grown to a staff of more than fifty outdoor educators in programs that are renowned nationwide, John Page remains the original from which the mold was cast and a unique memory to thousands of youths to whom he introduced the delights of simply messing about in boats.

The book picks up where the traditional Bay cruising guides leave off—where the open Bay merges into that marvelous edge of marsh and shallow water with winding tidal creeks that if unraveled would extend for more than 8,000 miles. This edge is where the Chesapeake's character lies—where the great blue herons, the ospreys and eagles and soft crabs and black ducks hang out. It is where the Bay is most accessible to nearly all of us, requiring only a small, economical watercraft—or just a pair of hipboots or old sneakers and a willingness to get muddy. Here is territory enough that a lifetime wouldn't be enough to investigate it all, although John Page comes as close as anyone.

To explore this realm of the Chesapeake, there is no better guide. Primarily a book about exploring the Bay, it is also a treatise on how to travel through any stretch of country, plugging all the senses into nature's multiple levels. The author embodies what Aldo Leopold, the conservationist and writer of *Sand County Almanac,* once called "a refined taste in natural objects." He is elegantly attuned to the ecosystem—the plants and animals and fish, and how they vary and change to the movement of tide and time of day, with the seasons and the salinity. His discourse ranges from the near-microscopic life of the creeks to how it all fits into the 64,000-square-mile drainage basin that is the Chesapeake Bay watershed, extending across six states, from Cooperstown, New York, nearly to North Carolina.

For all its scope, this is a practical book, written by a man who has the patience to spend hours "picking apart," as he puts it, a single small fishing hole, conducting analysis first with a depth-finder, then with a fishing rod, and finally with an expertly hurled cast net. So you will find here, in addition to beauty and philosophy, solid information about the kind of boat you need, the best bug repellent, where you can avoid sea nettles, and how to keep grass shrimp alive for bait. The section on the nearly lost art of poling a boat—so appropriate in a body of water whose average depth is less than twenty-two feet—is worth the price of admission.

The best advice in the book, however, is to get out there and see the Bay for yourself. John Page Williams is a fisherman, but he's at his best hooking people on the Chesapeake Bay, and this book is choice bait.

Tom Horton

Acknowledgments

Many watermen, fishing guides, research scientists, and wildlife biologists have shared their knowledge generously with me over the years. They know who they are. I owe them my deepest appreciation. Special thanks are due to Bill Portlock and Janet Harvey; to the Rev. Albert Jones of Reedville, who first taught me about precision fishing; to George Squires, late chairman of the English Department at St. Christopher's School in Richmond and son of the Northern Neck, who taught me to write a sentence; to Ellen Thorson of Annapolis Word Works for a mountain of typing; to Donna Malloy Smith of the Chesapeake Bay Foundation for help with graphics; and to my wife Louise, for her encouragement and support throughout the project.

*To my father, who started me out on these rivers
and creeks, and to the Chesapeake Bay Foundation,
which gave me a professional excuse
to explore them further.*

Part One

POKIN' AROUND

one

Introduction

It was a beautiful March day on the Patuxent: calm, clear, sunny, and warm. Two friends and I put the boat overboard and moved downriver from Selby's Landing. Small flocks of geese and ducks traded up and down the river. Yellowlegs and snipe poked through the stubble on the marshes. The water temperature was 8°C (46°F).

In the first hole of Mattaponi Creek, one of us cast a small lure and let it drift with the current. He smiled as the line jumped and the rod bent over. A big school of yellow perch was holding in the deep water, getting ready to ascend the creek to spawn. He landed the fish, and we headed upstream to have a look at the creek. It had been three months since any of us had been on it, and there was a lot to catch up on. I poled the skiff into a side tributary and stopped there to watch a pair of bluebirds in an alder shrub. As I did, four beautiful ducks, hooded mergansers, got up from a cove and flew just over us.

We really did not have a destination in mind, and a quick trip was not our intention. We edged the boat up onto the marsh and stepped onto very moist, spongy soil. The area was almost devoid of vegetation, and I thought about how different it would look in July, with plants growing 'way above our heads. To some people, the empty marsh would appear a wasteland, but we saw a few signs of the approaching spring. Still, the land was a lot slower to wake up than the creek.

We slipped up the creek with the tide to another deep hole full of perch and spent a couple of hours with our binoculars and fishing rods. Yellow perch are neither big nor ferocious, but they certainly are good to eat. These were all prime ten- to twelve-inch fish, golden yellow with dark olive bars and bright orange belly fins. We kept a dozen and gently released the rest.

At midday we moved down to a south-facing bank where the water had warmed to 13°C (55°F). As we drifted around a bend, a stocky, well-fed largemouth bass sucked in one of our lures. A marsh hawk dipped low over the marsh, foraging for mice. In midchannel, a painted turtle bobbed its head. We towed a small plankton net behind the boat for five minutes, and it came up loaded with copepods. These are tiny crustaceans that feed on plant and animal detritus (debris) washing out of the winter marshes. In turn they provide food for most of the small fish in the creek, including larval perch. Toward three o'clock, we headed back to the landing, deeply contented.

What did we have to show for our day? We hadn't conquered a wilderness—Mattaponi Creek is less than twenty miles from the U.S. Capitol. Our fish were good ones, but they weren't trophies. We hadn't seen any rare birds. Yet, for each of us, the day produced the kind of memories that can bring a smile and a fresh burst of energy anytime anywhere. It was a day to treasure, an investment of great and lasting value.

My friends and I had worked hard to enter the Mattaponi Creek community, to be part of it for a day. We had done our homework and put up with some windy, cold, rainy days on other trips. They were very much a part of the background against which we saw this one. Our excuse to the world was that we were fishing, but we were looking at everything: tides, bottom contours, marsh stubble, temperature, salinity, birds, small fish, large fish, plankton, humans. We were there to see if the winter had changed the creek dramatically. We knew that the bluebirds were courting, that the waterfowl were getting ready to head for the Canadian tundra and prairies, and that the yellowlegs had just come in from South America. They all do those things every year, but that fact doesn't blunt the value of the achievements, or the sense of wonder they evoke in the observer.

There were unpredictable elements too. After two years of drought, Mattaponi had seen a great deal of freshwater runoff. Sand, mud, and fallen trees had all been moved around. We didn't know till we threw our lines overboard whether we had hit the perch run correctly. We didn't know till the day before whether we'd have sun and calm or rain and screaming wind.

We did know that we were plugging ourselves into the system, ready to be grateful for whatever it had to offer us. We talk in metaphor about "being in tune with the river." In some sense known to some wise psychologist, something deep inside us was resonating with Mattaponi. We were part of the creek that day, participants in its biological community, at once observers and top-level predators. Cleaning the perch carefully back at the dock and eating them the next day was very much a part of the experience. We were reverent meat-fishermen.

One needn't know a waterway as well as we know Mattaponi, though, to find it exciting. One needn't be a trained naturalist, either. There is another metaphor, "Listening to the creek tell its story." It is a nice phrase, layered like an onion, as many good ideas are. What it means, first off, is observing, watching, and listening carefully to whatever is going on at the moment. Anyone can do that. It takes patience, not training.

As one watches, questions begin to form. Why are all those small fish up this creek? What draws hundreds of ducks and geese into this particular marsh? Now it will be useful to get out a couple of field guides and learn one or two of the most common species. A little background reading will offer some general principles about how these pieces fit together. Understanding comes at different levels. For anyone, experienced or not, it is exciting when things start to make sense. It is a thrill to realize that those ducks are in the marsh because the wild rice and smartweed that grow there produce tons of seeds. After exploring half a dozen of the Bay's big rivers, it will be just as exciting to begin to see patterns of similarity between marsh plant communities on all of them. At any level of experience, the sense of discovery is valid and something to treasure.

At the beginning of this kind of observing, it is a good idea to pick one area and spend some time exploring it. Several experiences will give you a fundamental sense of community structure. Coming to this basic sense is a satisfying process, and it offers a background against which to see the unusual. A river otter swimming down a creek is a sight worth seeing anytime, but it is more exciting if you realize how seldom these animals reveal themselves to people.

With a sense of the system, it is also interesting to watch one season give way to another. On the Chesapeake, each season has its own character and charm. The first small crabs of spring, the blooming marsh flowers of summer, the return of geese and ducks in fall, and the fat oysters of winter are all part of the fabric of a year.

Against this background, exploring new territory also is exciting. The Chesapeake is blessed abundantly with rivers, creeks, and marsh guts. There are remarkable patterns of similarity and difference among them. There is a great deal of water out there to watch and be part of.

I find myself writing this book out of the excitement and adventure I have found operating educational field trips for the Chesapeake Bay Foundation. My friend and former colleague at CBF, Bill Portlock, has illustrated it with photographs born of the same excitement and adventure, and Janet Harvey, who also once worked for CBF, has added descriptions of two of her favorite waters (the Gunpowder River and Kings Creek). We hope that the book will be a useful reference for anyone interested in spending time around the Cheaspeake's shoreline. We hope we are able to pass on some of the joy and wonder we find day to day as we work to be part of the Bay community.

two

The Chesapeake Bay

An Overview

To understand the Chesapeake system, first think of it as a big river. That's what it is—one of the largest river systems in the United States. In terms of freshwater discharge to an ocean, only the Columbia and the Mississippi are larger.

The Bay is actually the tidal mouth of the Susquehanna, which by itself is far and away the largest river on the Atlantic Coast of the United States. In terms again of freshwater discharge, it is larger than the Connecticut (the second largest) and the Hudson (the third) combined. That statement always draws stares in conversation, but we tend to think of the Hudson as we know it, say, from crossing the Tappan Zee Bridge. That bridge spans the river well down in its tidal section. For a comparable place on the Chesapeake, it would be like driving across from Windmill Point to Onancock. We think of the Susquehanna where Interstate 95 crosses it at Havre de Grace, where it is only a mile across, but the comparable point on the Hudson is well above Albany, where the river is much smaller. Closer to home, one can think of the Potomac at its mouth, seven miles across, but the point on the Potomac that compares with what we call the mouth of the Susquehanna is actually up at the Key Bridge, between Arlington and Georgetown.

The Indians, without meaning to, played a trick on us when they decided that the big river should have one name, *Susquehanna*, while the estuary down below it should have another, *Chesapeake*. Their brethren on the Potomac did not make the same distinction, giving that river the same name all the way from its source in the mountains down to where it joins the Bay.

It is much easier to think of the Chesapeake as one system by going back to the end of the last ice age, some 15,000 years ago. At this point, sea level was about 100 meters (330 feet) lower than it is today. The coastline was out near the continental shelf, and the mouth of the Susquehanna was at what today we call Norfolk Canyon, a groove on the continental shelf off the Virginia Capes.

At this time, the Susquehanna ran all the way down from the edge of the Wisconsin Glacier, in what is now north-central Pennsylvania, picking up a number of large tributaries from the eastern slopes of the Appalachians, the Blue Ridge, and the edge of the Allegheny Plateau. Thus the big rivers that we know today as the James and the Potomac, plus the smaller ones like the Rappahannock, the York, and the Patuxent, all flowed into the Susquehanna as it made its way down to the sea. The Eastern Shore rivers drained into the Susquehanna in much the same way they do into the Bay today.

As the glacier began to melt, the sea level rose, and the Atlantic pushed its way back into the mouth of the great river and up its valley. Eight thousand years ago, tidal water reached up to where Smith Island is today. Five thousand years ago, it reached Betterton on the upper Eastern Shore, and 3,000 years ago the Susquehanna Flats. Since that time, of course, the flats have enlarged as the river has dropped tons upon tons of sediment onto them.

Sea level appears to be rising again. None of us will be around a hundred years from now, but there is some speculation that by that time there will be noticeable changes in the shape of the Bay's shoreline.

In any case, the result of all this geologic activity is a broad, generally shallow body of water through which some forty major rivers find a common path to the ocean. As estuaries go, it is unusual in that it has not only a major river to feed its main stem, but also other large rivers which join it down in its tidal portions. Its forty tidal rivers are further subdivided into several hundred creeks and countless coves. The result is a huge number of areas for the small boat explorer to search out and investigate.

The mechanics of the Bay system are worth a basic discussion, for they make it what it is, an extraordinarily rich body of water—not only a great cruising ground but a wonderful producer of seafood, and home to wildlife which delight both the eye and the ear. Remember that the Bay is a shallow pan whose bottom lies below sea level. The same holds true for all the tidal tributaries. The point on each at which its bed reaches sea level is called the fall line. Notice too that while the ocean flows into this shallow pan through the mouth at the Virginia Capes, fresh water flows down all the tributary rivers and streams into it as well. Thus the Chesapeake system is a mixing ground for fresh and salt water.

Notice also that as each river reaches sea level, it widens out and the incoming tides begin to retard its flow twice a day. A great deal of whatever is carried down the rivers settles out in these tidal reaches, including sediments of various sizes and organic material of all sorts. The Bay is a sink, a catchment for its rivers. There is a net outflow from it to the Atlantic, but it is much slower than the rivers' inflows to it, so a great deal accumulates in it. Much of what comes down the rivers and settles in the Bay's tidal waters is food for microorganisms or scavengers, or plant nutrients that can fuel the growth of phytoplankton and submerged grasses. Estuaries by nature are rich bodies of water, natural food traps. The quantity of seafood which a healthy one can produce is staggering.

Given the fact that the Bay can produce large quantities of food, it is useful to look again at its flow characteristics, because they are more complex than one might otherwise guess and because that very complexity is quite useful to many of the creatures that live there. Fresh water is less dense than salt, and the density varies directly with salinity. When fresh water flows down the rivers, it floats over the seawater that comes in from the ocean. The actual patterns that develop depend a great deal on the geometry of the river basins, the strength of the tides as determined by the moon and the wind, and the fresh water coming down the rivers.

It is easy enough to see how the whole process can be very complicated, and in fact when physical oceanographers try to describe the fluid dynamics, the mathematical equations involved are enough to make mere mortals weep. It is, however, simple enough for us mortals to understand that at any point in the Bay, and in most of the tidal portions of the rivers, the water is saltier at the bottom than it is at the top.

There is another joker in the deck: the Coriolis force that develops from the earth's rotation, which tends in this hemisphere to push higher-density water to the east. Thus seawater that comes in on the tides through the Virginia Capes hugs the Eastern Shore of Virginia as it flows north, while the freshwater flow out of the Susquehanna, Potomac, and other big rivers tends to hug the western shore. The same pattern can be seen in maps of salinity profiles of the rivers, and it can even be seen in the sediment plumes on satellite images of the whole Bay. In general, then, as one crosses the Bay from west to east, the water will be fresher to the west and saltier to the east.

Where the fresh and salt waters mix, there is turbulence between the layers. Waves of salt water form, intruding upward into the freshwater layer. The freshwater layer picks up these waves and carries them back downstream with the river flow. Thus the surface waters never stay completely fresh, and there is enough mixing from the turbulence between the layers to keep bottom water diluted somewhat in all areas except down near the Bay's mouth.

As salty water is picked up and carried downstream by the fresh surface currents, seawater flows in through the mouth of the Bay from the Atlantic to replace it. This pattern is partially reversed twice a day by the tides, but there is a net movement of water *up* the Bay at the bottom. At the same time, even though rising tides bring fresh water back up the Bay some of the time at the surface, there is a net movement *down* the Bay at the surface. Thus there is a two-way escalator system that works in the rivers and in the main stem of the Bay itself. The idea may sound fantastic, but it has been going on for at least 15,000 years. If you were to guess that a number of the Bay's animals have learned to use this escalator system over the course of that time, you would be right. It is a superb transportation system that connects every nook and cranny of the tidal Chesapeake system with the continental shelf. The comings and goings on it stagger the imagination. As you read on, you will pick up hints of a few of them.

To complicate matters a little more, not all of a tidal river has salty water at the bottom. In the big rivers especially, freshwater flow is strong enough that it keeps the wedge of intruding salt water pushed a few miles downstream below the fall line. The freshwater section between the wedge and the fall line is referred to as the tidal fresh section of the river. These areas are some of the least noticed waterways in the Bay country, and they are fascinating. The reasons why will be obvious in the description of them that follows.

Tidal fresh waters are strongly affected by the tides, producing what seem to be most peculiar characteristics. The height of the tide change is generally determined by the shape of the river basin. Some of the strongest tides in the Bay are well up the rivers in tidal fresh sections. In fact, the highest average tide change in the entire Bay system (3.9 feet) is at Walkerton on the Mattaponi River, some seventy miles above the mouth of the York, right in the middle of tidal fresh waters. See the Trip Description in Chapter 11.

Tidal flows in these areas are often asymmetrical. That is, the current may run out for seven hours and back in for five and a half, due to strong downstream flows from the upper watershed. Tidal currents in these river sections do not necessarily reverse after they have reached maximum height. Remember that a tide is a long-period wave with crests travelling approximately twelve hours twenty-five minutes apart. High tide is simply the passage of the wave peak, but water may continue to flow in the same direction after the peak has passed.

The flows in these areas can be quite complex. Don't try to understand them all at once. Simply watch what happens and file the information away. If you spend some time on the rivers, patterns will start to emerge.

Most of us who work on the Bay professionally come to our jobs because we love wildlife, whether we are fishermen, hunters, bird-watchers, or all of the above. At first, physical oceanography seems a dry and irrelevant subject. Even geology appears unimportant. Who could get interested in mud and sand and gravel when there are crabs and oysters and rockfish and Canada geese and great blue herons and ospreys to pay attention to? As should be obvious by now, I have learned otherwise. The physical dynamics of this system have a great deal to do with why it is the way it is. They push a great deal of sand and mud and gravel around. These sediments grow hundreds of thousands of acres of luxuriant marshes. The marshes vary with the salinity, but the rich soils on which they are based furnish food and habitat for a host of invertebrates, fish, amphibians, reptiles, birds, and mammals. They will figure heavily in the chapters to follow.

I don't love fish and birds any less now. Instead I appreciate the Bay more for the rich and complex system it is. There is enough out there to keep me fascinated for the rest of my life. I wish you the same.

Areas to Explore in Small Boats

Tidal Fresh Rivers

When we think of the Chesapeake, we somehow have conditioned ourselves to see broad open waters and salt marshes. With all due regard to those areas, the small boat explorer is missing a good bet if he/she neglects the upper tidal rivers. They are rich. Read on, but best of all, go see for yourself.

As noted above, the term *tidal fresh* refers to the section of a river where its bed first reaches sea level and becomes affected by the tides.

If freshwater flow coming downstream is much less than saltwater flow on incoming tides, the freshwater flow will be overpowered immediately, and the entire tidal section will be brackish. Broad rivers with very small watersheds, like the Severn on the upper western shore, work this way. On the other hand, a river with a large watershed and a heavy freshwater flow, like the Rappahannock or the Choptank, will have a long zone in which that flow pushes back the salt water of incoming tides. The fresh water fills the channel completely for a surprising distance downstream from the fall line before allowing penetration by the tongue of deep salt water that sets up the Bay system's characteristic two-layered flow.

Rainfall patterns, varying as they do from year to year and month to month, continually change the length of the tidal fresh zones, and the plants and animals in the rivers must adjust accordingly. It is, however, possible to describe an average. Thus the upper Bay itself is basically tidal but fresh for some miles, from Smith's Falls on the Susquehanna down to Pooles Island, near Baltimore. The Potomac is tidal fresh for about thirty-five miles, from Little Falls down to Quantico. The James is fresh from the fall line at Richmond about fifty miles down below the mouth of the Chickahominy to Jamestown.

These three rivers have by far the largest watersheds in the Chesapeake system (over 80 percent among them) and thus the longest tidal fresh sections, but many others have significant tidal fresh water as well. Some examples are listed below:

Upper Bay—Since the Bay itself is basically fresh here, all the tributaries are tidal fresh. Good examples for the small boat explorer include Swan Creek (off the Susquehanna Flats), Otter Point Creek (Bush River), Seneca and Dundee creeks, the Gunpowder River, the Northeast River, the Elk River, the Bohemia River, Still Pond Creek, and the Sassafras River.

Eastern Shore
Chester River—from Millington downstream to Deep Landing.
Choptank River—from Greensboro downstream to Ganey's Wharf, including the entire Tuckahoe Creek system, plus the heads of Kings Creek, Miles Creek, and Hunting Creek.
Blackwater River—the section above the Blackwater refuge; also the Little Blackwater down to the refuge.
Transquaking River—the section down to Bestpitch Ferry, including the entire Chicamacomico River.

Nanticoke River—from Seaford, Delaware, downstream to Vienna, including all of Broad and Marshyhope creeks, plus the heads of Chicone Creek, Barren Creek, Rewastico Creek, and Quantico Creek.

Wicomico River—downriver to Upper Ferry.

Manokin River—from Princess Anne downstream to the mouth of Kings Creek, including all of Kings Creek.

Pocomoke River—from Porter's Crossing, above Snow Hill, down to Rehobeth, plus the upper end of Pitts Creek.

Western Shore

Patuxent River—from Wayson's Corner (Hill's Bridge at Rt. 4) downstream to Nottingham, plus the upper ends of Hall Creek, Cocktown Creek, Black Swamp Creek, and Little Hunting Creek.

Potomac River—from Little Falls to Quantico, plus the upper parts of Aquia Creek, Potomac Creek, Nanjemoy Creek, the Wicomico River (Allens Fresh), Breton Bay, Upper Machodoc Creek, Rosier Creek, Mattox Creek, Nomini Creek, and the St. Marys River.

Rappahannock River—from Fredericksburg downstream to Portobago Bay, plus the upper ends of Jetts Creek, Occupacia Creek, Cat Point Creek, Mount Landing Creek, Hoskins Creek, Piscataway Creek, and Totuskey Creek.

Piankatank River—Dragon Run from Saluda (Rt. 17 bridge) to Freeport.

York River—the Pamunkey and Mattaponi rivers from Rt. 360 downstream nearly to West Point, plus the upper ends of Poropotank Creek and Taskinas Creek (York River State Park).

James River—from Lee Bridge (Rt. 1) in Richmond downstream to Jamestown, including the entire Chickahominy River from Walkers Dam (Lanexa) down and the Appomattox River from Petersburg down.

In general, these rivers and their creeks are narrow and winding. They tend to funnel the wind directly either upstream or downstream. As noted, their tides are strong. The curves are called meanders, and they can be remarkably regular. Strange as it may seem, these curves represent the most efficient form for the river to assume, minimizing friction between its bed and the water for this combination of tides and strong downstream flow. As the curves develop, the water flowing around the outsides accelerates and erodes those banks, creating deep holes with steep sides and hard sand or gravel bottoms. On the insides, the currents slow down and the lightest sediments (fine silt particles) settle out, creating shallow, soft-bottomed flats. A depth-sounder can teach a lot here.

Once the effects of river flow, meanders, tides, and winds are added up, the result is winding rivers with steep wooded banks alternating with broad marshes. Narrow feeder creeks often enter as the rivers change direction and the high banks give way to marshes. Part of the charm here for the small boat explorer is that there is always something new to see or a new creek to explore around the next turn. A few houses perch up on the high banks, a few docks and an occasional public landing stand at the water's edge.

On most of the rivers there are few commercial facilities. In some areas, there are remnants of old commercial wharves. Up until the early 1930s, steamboats served the communities on all these waterways. Lumber, produce, and other goods travelled by schooner. It is a source of constant amazement to think about the tight places that the captains of old could get their ships into.

Before them, the Indians found the tidal fresh rivers rich hunting, fishing, and foraging grounds. Archeologists, both professional and amateur, have documented a large number of sites.

Today, there is little commercial activity. The three big rivers have some shipping, and the Nanticoke, Pocomoke, and Rappahannock have some as well. A few savvy watermen make their living catching catfish, turtles, eels, and carp. There are some water-skiers in season. Perhaps the biggest crowds come from bass fishing tournaments. By and large the rivers are uncrowded.

The great numbers of flora and fauna in tidal fresh rivers are wonderful. Fresh water allows a diversity of plants that is impossible farther downstream where salt concentrations are higher. The marshes may have over twenty plant species, against seven or eight in a downriver salt marsh. Trees will vary from ash, maple, black gum, and cypress in the bottomlands to huge beech and scarlet oaks on the high banks. A pull of a minnow seine in August may pick up fifteen different species, including both local animals like spottail shiners and summer visitors from the lower Bay, like juvenile menhaden and crabs.

The tidal fresh marshes deserve special consideration. Along the edges of the waterways are broadleaf plants like yellow pond lily, pickerelweed, arrow arum, and American three-square. These marshes are flooded regularly by the tides. Behind them, at slightly higher soil elevations, are wild rice, smartweeds, tearthumb, Walter's millet, cat-tails, great bulrush, and river bulrush.

All have substantial value as wildlife foods. The first four groups produce great quantities of nutritious seeds for waterfowl and other birds. The Bay country has the second heaviest concentration of wild rice in the United States, after the marshes of Minnesota and Wisconsin. Even so, the smartweeds and tearthumb produce more tonnage of seed, and they ripen at a most appropriate time for the ducks that arrive in late fall. The stalks of cattails and the bulrushes have tasty, tender hearts that offer excellent food for muskrats.

A number of wildflowers also grow in the tidal fresh marshes, including marsh hibiscus, cardinal flower, New York ironweed, and tickseed sunflower. At the back edges of the marshes, on higher, firmer, but still wet swamp soils, are shrubs like alder (an important beaver food and construction material) and viburnum.

The list is abbreviated, and the community changes constantly from mid-April till frost. See "The Seasons" below for patterns to notice and Gene Silberhorn's *Common Marsh Plants of the Mid-Atlantic Coast* for more information on individual species.

As mentioned above, the fauna of the rivers is quite varied, especially in late summer and fall. Local predators like largemouth bass, chain pickerel, and channel catfish often turn up with belliesful of prey like juvenile spot and menhaden that have been spawned on the continental shelf, out in the Atlantic. Other travelers include river herring (alewives) and blueback herring, which ascend the rivers to spawn in spring but spend the bulk of their lives in the ocean (though their young stay in the rivers their first summer), and blue crabs, which hatch in the lower Bay but move up the rivers all the way to the fall lines to live and grow. White and yellow perch spawn in early spring up the rivers and creeks, and then they spread throughout the rivers for the rest of the year, with the whites ranging down even to the midrange salinities. Both species are, unfortunately, experiencing spawning difficulties, as are the shad and rockfish (striped bass) which also spawn up the rivers but live primarily in the Atlantic (shad) or in both the open Bay and the Atlantic (rock). Other locals include carp (some of which are huge), shiner minnows, and even a species of large sucker, the northern redhorse. Several small fish move up and down the rivers, in the process offering forage to all predators. They include silversides, anchovies, and hogchokers (small flounder— our only native sole). The two Bay field guides in the "Books" section in Chapter 4 can supply details of individual species' life cycles.

Several reptile species frequent the tidal fresh rivers: redbelly turtles, painted turtles, mud turtles, and snapping turtles. The first three can often be seen sunning themselves on logs in warm weather. The snappers are less obtrusive, generally staying in deeper water. It is unusual to come across them unless you set some sort of trap. Still, there are plenty of them around, and they are dangerous if aroused, but it is easy to stay out of their way.

The only common snakes are the northern water snake, which is always curious and feisty when cornered, and the black rat snake, which does not swim but comes down to the back edges of the marshes. Neither is poisonous, and bites are quite unlikely unless you deliberately handle the animals. Still, a bite should be treated immediately for infection, and the victim should have an up-to-date tetanus shot. Copperheads are very rare, but they should be treated with great caution if encountered. They are generally not aggressive; nevertheless you should give them a wide berth.

Birds of all sorts live in tidal fresh marshes, from songbirds like the ubiquitous red-winged blackbirds and the spectacular prothonotary warblers of the cypress swamps to large waterfowl like Canada geese and tundra swans, to wading birds like great blue herons, shorebirds like spotted sandpipers, and raptors like ospreys. These rivers are also excellent eagle habitat. It is always worth keeping an eye to the sky.

Mammals include the prolific muskrat, the beaver, the raccoon, and the river otter. Muskrats live here in huge numbers. Their huts are evident in the fall. Beavers have made a strong comeback in recent years. They have been, in fact, too successful at projects like damming creeks and thus closing off perch spawning runs. State game agencies stay busier than they would like trapping and transplanting the animals. Raccoons are adaptable and do very well feeding on everything from worms in the high marsh to persimmons at the edges of the swamps. Otters are more common than most of us realize. They hunt large territories and eat fish straight through the year. They are very good at keeping out of sight of people. Tracks on the beach are often blurred. Usually the only way to identify an otter's trail is to find its characteristic scats (droppings)—fish scales and bones. They are magnificent wild animals, and it is always a thrill to see them.

As noted, seasonal change is dramatic on tidal fresh rivers. Check the sections of this chapter on the subject. Be careful on these rivers, especially in cold weather. Banks are frequently either soft or steep, dropoffs are often sudden, tides and currents are strong, thunderstorms can pop up suddenly in warm weather, and facilities are few and far between. But go and get to know them. They offer a rich fabric for the careful observer, and they tend to be less crowded than other Bay waterways. They are delights in every season.

Brackish Rivers

For most of us, the first image of a tidal creek that comes to mind is a brackish one—short, wide, ringed with a fringe of cordgrass, backed up by wooded banks alternating with a few houses and docks. It is summer, and someone is poling a skiff along the edge looking for soft crabs. Schools of young menhaden dimple the surface. An osprey sits on a nest atop a channel marker.

The term brackish river covers a broad variety of water, from the creeks around the Eastern Neck National Wildlife Refuge, at the mouth of the Chester River, where the salinity is less than 30 percent that of seawater, to Mobjack Bay, in Gloucester and Mathews counties, where the salinity is over 70 percent of seawater. In general, these waterways are bordered by gently rolling or very flat lands that lend themselves well to people and houses. They are, in fact, the areas of which Captain John Smith said, "Heaven and earth never framed a better place for man's habitation."

The brackish rivers and creeks are immediately inviting. They can be rough in windy weather and should always be treated with extra caution when the water is cold, but they typify the pastoral, human-scale Chesapeake settings that boatmen have loved for centuries. In warm weather, they hum with life, much of it young and busy growing up. There is no better kind of waterway to begin studying the natural history of the Bay system. Species are few and abundant. The half-dozen marsh plant species all will be interesting ones that are important to the system. If the Bay as a whole is too big to grasp at first, the marshes are great places to "sidle up to it" (words courtesy of Captain Tom Horton, one of the Bay's best friends and writers).

The marshes will be primarily fringes and pockets, with only a few large expanses but with enough bits and pieces to add up to substantial acreage. The dominant plant will be saltmarsh cordgrass, which grows in the intertidal zone where it is flooded twice a day by the tides. This valuable grass makes great contributions of both food and habitat on the brackish rivers. Behind it, at elevations that are flooded only on spring and storm tides, grow saltmeadow hay (a close relative of saltmarsh cordgrass), saltgrass, saltmarsh bulrush, and giant cordgrass (another relative). At the uppermost extreme are two woody shrubs, marsh elder and groundsel tree. *Common Marsh Plants of the Mid-Atlantic Coast* will give you good insight to this plant community and its overall importance to the rivers and the Bay.

The fact that these areas with such a wide salinity range can be lumped together reflects the fact that the plants and animals are species that can adapt to wide changes in salt concentration. Not only does salinity change as one moves downriver or down-Bay, but it changes with seasons, depending on rainfall patterns. Closer to the mouth of the Bay, oceanic species of fish and birds are more common, and they spread farther up the Bay in dry years; however, the majority of the plants and animals in the brackish rivers are the ones like cordgrasses, white perch, menhaden, and blue crabs that can adapt to a broad range of salinities. These most adaptable creatures have a real competitive edge in such difficult waters, and they do very well indeed. The half-dozen plant species are remarkably prolific, growing a great biomass of food to fuel the river. Healthy brackish rivers can produce tremendous numbers of fish and shellfish, with plenty of birdlife around as well.

These areas are subtle. It takes more than one or two trips to the marshes to figure them out. They're worth watching day after day, year after year. Currents, for example, are still important, but their movements are much less obvious than those in a narrow tidal fresh river. In those waters, it is fun to try to figure out how flow and tide shape the channels, and often the careful observer can do so, but the wider brackish rivers are much more difficult to understand. Still, the lack of obvious pattern is no reason not to watch. A depth-sounder is still a useful piece of gear, and learning how to read details like fish schools and bottom composition will enrich one's sense of what is below the surface.

Because these rivers and creeks usually have at least a few houses on them, the birds and other animals have learned to be unobtrusive in their habits, with the exception of the very adaptable seagulls, terns, and crows. They are certainly worth watching—their behavior is more complex than that of the other water birds—but the real joys for the small boat cruiser are the great blue herons that stalk the shallows and the ospreys that fish the open waters. The herons are around almost all year, leaving in winter only when the water ices over and in late spring to nest in one of the Bay's rookeries. The ospreys are on the Bay from March till September, when they depart for their "other summer" in Central and South America.

Other birds enrich the brackish rivers. A number of these bodies of water have eagle nests, and transient eagles use them as well. The Bay's eagle population has rebounded strongly since DDT was banned in 1972.

On the Rappahannock, the reach below Horsehead Point and Wilmot Wharf is great eagle territory. Photo by Bill Portlock.

It is worth reading a good bird field guide carefully to learn how to identify an eagle soaring. There are several field marks to use, so the process is not difficult. It's a fair bet that the Bay system has at least 300 eagles scattered around it on any given day of the year, so the odds of seeing one sooner or later are very good indeed. Several trips described later are good eagle locations. These are good places to start learning to see the birds.

In fall, winter, and early spring, the brackish rivers host thousands of waterfowl. Perhaps the most conspicuous are Canada geese, whose numbers have mushroomed in the past forty years. The Bay is host also to one of the largest winter populations of tundra swans in the United States. The big white birds are magnificent features of the Bay in cold weather. Besides geese and swans, some twenty other species of waterfowl winter on the Bay and its tributaries. For the careful observer, they become fascinating focal points during the colder months.

One other cold weather visitor deserves note. The Bay country is home in the fall and spring to hundreds of loons that have come down from northern waterways (mostly Michigan and Ontario). The birds winter in the Atlantic off the Delmarva coast. When they are on the Chesapeake, the loons flock together in groups of from half a dozen to over a hundred, and the flocks will sometimes chase baitfish just like schools of bluefish and rockfish, complete with gulls diving on the leftover scraps. One loon-watching note is in order, though. From October through March, the birds are in winter plumage, which is quite different from their bold summer pattern. Again, check the field guides for details.

This short list is meant only to whet the appetite. The notes that follow on the seasons will suggest other birds of interest.

Most of the Bay's mammals are smart enough to stay out of peoples' way. Raccoons, muskrats, and river otters are all numerous. They are, however, active primarily at night and around dawn and dusk. Still, a sharp-eyed observer will see plenty of evidence of their presence.

The most obvious sign of muskrat activity in warm weather is floating sprigs of cordgrass. The bases of the stalks will have been chopped out at acute angles by the animals' sharp teeth. Muskrats are unobtrusive, but once one's consciousness is attuned to them, they seem to show up everywhere. In cold weather, their lodges are also obvious signs. From time to time, the observer will see the animals themselves, chugging along like little brown steamboats.

Coons are opportunistic omnivores, as noted above. On the brackish rivers, they will eat anything from ripe persimmons to clams dug up at low tide to fiddler crabs and fish, when they can catch them. The most obvious coon sign is tracks along the shore—long, slender toes with toenails. Though the animals are largely nocturnal, occasionally one will turn up foraging the edge of a creek during daytime.

River otters do well on brackish rivers, too. As noted above, there are a great many of them around the Bay and its tributaries, and they are magnificent, powerful wild animals. A family of otters may hunt a territory of fifty miles of shoreline over a week's time. That sounds like a lot of water, but with all the Bay's creeks and coves, it is shorter than it seems. On the brackish rivers they are fish eaters by preference but will eat crabs. Their tracks are shorter and squarer than those of coons, but those tracks are often obliterated on the shore by the otter's antics.

Instead of looking for tracks, the careful observer looks for a trail, an area of beach or marsh where grasses have been battered down or twisted and torn up. The otter's scats will be deposited on the trail.

There is a special thrill in learning to track a creature like an otter. Occasionally the tracker is rewarded by a glimpse of the animal swimming and diving. In winter, otters seem a little less cautious and may be seen playing on ice. At any season, seeing an otter is a treat.

Fish stocks on the brackish rivers are less diverse than in either high salinity areas or tidal fresh stretches. Forage fish include the ubiquitous silverside minnows, bay anchovies, menhaden, killifish, and hogchokers. White perch live comfortably at salinities up to fifteen parts per thousand (about half that of seawater), so they turn up on most of the rivers (including the upper main stem of the Bay itself). Rockfish, which are highly adaptable, occur throughout the system. Fish that spawn on the continental shelf use much of the Bay in the summer and fall, but their young tend to use the upper reaches more readily than the adults. This loosely defined group includes spot, croakers (hardheads), gray trout, bluefish, and summer flounder. In general, the largest adults of each species occur near the mouth of the Bay, though trout and bluefish especially will move far up the Bay in dry years. Some adult bluefish apparently migrate up the Bay and out through the Chesapeake and Delaware Canal each year in May and June.

In August, a seine haul in a tidal fresh river may net fifteen species. Further down in the brackish part of the same river, the same seine may pick up only six, but the numbers of individuals may well be greater. What brackish rivers give up in diversity they often make up for in sheer tonnage of life. A healthy brackish river can teem with fish.

Frogs and other amphibians cannot tolerate appreciable salinity, and most reptiles cannot either. Water snakes are more land-bound on the brackish portions of the river, though they will forage the back edges of the marshes, as will blacksnakes and, rarely, copperheads. Painted, red-belly, and snapping turtles do not venture far downriver, but the diamond-back terrapin takes up where they leave off. This lovely animal, once threatened by overharvest for its succulent meat, is making a comeback on the Bay. It is common on most of the tidal rivers, though it is often unobserved. Like otters, terrapins see more of us than we of them. They bob close to the surface, with only their heads showing, and they duck below quickly if approached. Only in late spring are they obvious, as they congregate in marsh coves to mate. At that time, the observant boatman may spot fifty heads bobbing in a single cove, and fifty more of the terrapins up on the marsh banks. Either way, one head or fifty, it is good to see the diamondback doing better.

Over the past hundred years, the major economic value of the brackish rivers has been their production of crabs and oysters. As anyone who has read *Beautiful Swimmers* (see the "Books" section in Chapter 4) knows, the Chesapeake's crabs spawn in the main stem of the salty lower Bay, but they do their best growing in the brackish waters of the rivers and the upper main stem. Thus the Wye River and surrounding waters on the Upper Eastern Shore are the classic producers of the biggest males, No. 1 jimmies. As much as any other river in the system, the Wye is the one that attracts the largest number of recreational crabbers, as well as some very savvy commercial trotliners. But the Wye does not have a monopoly on big crabs. The middle reaches of every tidal river grow them, from the Chester and the Severn in Maryland to Mobjack Bay's rivers in Virginia. The abundant life in the rivers forms a good food base for the omnivorous, scavenging crabs, and the variety of deep and shallow waters gives them habitat to shed their shells periodically, adjust to changing weather conditions, and mate.

A century ago, the Chesapeake's capacity to produce oysters seemed endless. For many years, river oysters were considered the best. Thus Patuxent oysters had their loyal following, as did those from the Chop-tank, the Potomac, and the Rappahannock. The James has always been known as the Bay's greatest producer of seed (juvenile) oysters. Its seed is used by both states in planting programs on public rocks (oyster grounds) in the main Bay and by private planters on leased bottom in the rivers and creeks.

In recent years, the Bay's oyster fisheries have been a shadow of their former selves. Management problems, overharvest, diseases, low oxygen in the summertime, and maybe a change in the Bay's phytoplankton community (the primary source of oyster food) all have contributed. The brackish rivers have experienced some troubling problems.

The source of those problems is the very mechanism that makes these rivers rich. They are traps. Fresh water flowing downstream from their watersheds suddenly comes into their wide basins and slows down. The incoming tides push against that water through the tidal fresh reaches, and that push helps to retard the flow even further. Thus net downstream flow in the brackish rivers is quite slow. There is variation from river to river and from season to season, but it is safe to say that much of what the fresh waters bring down the rivers stays in them.

What the rivers suffer from at this period in their history in over-enrichment. They are too fertile, suffering from too much of a good thing. That statement sounds like a contradiction, but the condition is one suffered by most waterways with lots of people living around them.

There is a later section of this chapter on overenrichment and the other problems facing the Bay (see "Problems and Possibilities" below). They are serious, but do not be discouraged by them. The rest of this chapter is bait, meant to entice you, the reader, to explore brackish rivers and other Bay waterways. Be assured that there is still plenty to love. Fishing may be tougher in some of the rivers, and it is difficult to make a living oystering, but the small boat explorer can still catch fish and crabs, buy oysters in season at the docks, watch ospreys raise their young, and marvel at the beauty of the cordgrass. Go. Soon.

Salt Marshes

Broad, open expanses of high-salinity salt marsh are usually laced with tidal guts that are just right for exploring in small boats. Access to some of them is difficult because it means crossing wide stretches of open water, but those that can be reached without undue exposure to wind and waves are well worth the effort.

In this category, the Big Salt Marsh at Poquoson, below the York River, is a favorite (see trip description in Chapter 11), but there are other good ones as well. On the western shore, they include the marshes around the Hole in the Wall at the eastern end of Gwynn's Island, the Grandview Natural Preserve at the mouth of Back River in Hampton, and the Ragged

In suitable weather a big salt marsh is perfect for exploring by canoe, kayak, or rowboat. This could be anywhere, but it happens to be just below the Potomac looking south from the mouth of the Great Wicomico. Photo by Bill Portlock.

Island Creek marsh at the mouth of the James River across from Newport News. On the Eastern Shore, Janes Island State Park and the Cedar Island marsh just outside Crisfield, the marshes on the east side of Pocomoke Sound below Saxis Island, and the ones at the mouths of creeks like Onancock, Nandua, and Occohannock to the south are all good for the prudent small boat explorer to consider. See the trip description sections in later chapters for further information.

It would seem that with their high salinity these marshes should be harsh places, but in fact the salinity here is more stable (at 60 to 90 percent that of seawater) than on most of the brackish rivers, so it is actually easier to cope with for those plants and animals that are adapted to it. The cordgrass and other saltmarsh plants described in the brackish river section thrive here, as do several others, like sea lavender, that do not occur farther up the Bay.

Proximity to the ocean brings in some birds not seen farther north, like black skimmers, Louisiana herons, brown pelicans, and oystercatchers, along with standard species like ospreys and great blue herons. A surprising variety of juvenile fish occur here as well, making these areas great for pulling a minnow seine or throwing a cast net (see Chapter 4). Pack a good fish guide like McClane's (see the "Books" section in Chapter 4), and take a fishing rod too. As always, keep an eye out for otter trails.

Lower Bay salt marshes are exciting, especially in early and late summer. Be careful of your boat in broad exposed waters. Protect yourself carefully from the sun. Carry a good insect repellent (especially for no-see-ums, mosquitoes, sheep flies, and greenheads). Use prudence and common sense. But look for the excitement. This open, big-sky country is beautiful and rich in life.

The Seasons

If salinity is the environmental factor that primarily determines what plants and animals live on a particular waterway, then water temperature is the primary determinant of how they live at any one time. Most of the Bay's creatures are cold-blooded. That is, their body temperatures vary with the temperature of the water around them. Passage of the seasons has a great deal to do with what happens. Understanding the seasons and knowing what to look for on a given day afield will enrich your experiences immensely.

Spring

The story that begins this book tells of an early spring day on a tidal fresh river. Late February and early March are generally considered to be drab, dreary, and depressing in the Bay country, but they needn't be. Spring's thousands of rebirths and new beginnings seem like a succession of miracles after winter's cold. The season comes in a series of steps, over a period of three months. By exercising caution and some thought, the small boat explorer can string together a long chain of memorable days watching the Bay come back to life as the season progresses and water temperatures rise. To follow the onset of spring, it is important to understand two physical properties of water: specific heat and density. Both have profound effects on the Bay's plants and animals.

Water has a very high specific heat. This is a scientific way to say that it must absorb a great deal of heat to raise its temperature. Thus large bodies of water require much more heat to warm up than smaller ones do. The open Bay in mid-February is a very cold place, but a shallow cove with southern exposure on a tidal creek may warm up quite fast even under the weak February sun. Because of water's high specific heat, spring comes to the tidal fresh rivers first, then to the brackish waters of the lower rivers, and then to the open Bay.

Two major factors influence water density in the Chesapeake: temperature and salinity. Water is densest at 39.1°F (4°C). Thus winter's ice, at 32°F or less, floats over 34°F surface water, and bottom water may be warmer, at 38°F. But as the air begins to warm, the ice melts, the surface warms to 39.1°F, and it sinks, bringing bottom water to the surface. This exchange is called *turnover*, and it occurs in all temperate bodies of water as they warm in the spring and cool in the fall.

Late winter Bay water is very clear. Plankton populations are low. Turnover brings turbulence, and the bottom waters that come to the surface bring sediments with them, making the Bay, or river, or creek suddenly murky. Some of the murk is detritus (decayed plant and animal material) that has settled during the winter. These waters are also usually low in oxygen, since there has been little exchange with the surface over the winter. But now winds and rains reoxygenate the rich soup of detritus that comes up from the bottom, and runoff from the brown stubble of the marshes augments it.

As the water warms the soup, the population of detritus-eating zooplankton explodes. Copepods are especially abundant (up to 10,000 per cubic meter of water), and they are particularly important in spring, since they form a major food base for any animals able to take advantage of them, like larval and juvenile fish.

The other density factor is salinity. Remember the story of the Bay's origins in the first part of this chapter and the description of its two-layer mass transit system. Crabs and fish don't think about this up-and-down escalator system, but they use it. It plays a major role in the life cycles of most of the Bay's creatures, especially in spring.

Tidal Fresh Rivers—Fish that spawn in the spring start to stir around as soon as the rivers begin to warm in late February. The earliest to spawn in the tidal fresh rivers are the shiner minnows. They are followed quickly by the yellow perch, which spawn up in the creeks at water temperatures of about 45°F (7.2°C). The yellow perch run is generally considered by upper Bay fishermen to be the beginning of the new season, but yellow perch are not alone in prowling the rivers at this time. Chain pickerel and white perch are only a couple of weeks away from their spawning too, so they are active, and largemouth bass begin to feed in the shallows as well, though they will not spawn till late April and May. When the eggs of the shiners, both of the perch, and pickerel hatch, the larvae and juveniles feed heavily on the abundant copepods.

As the white perch run ends, other spawners move in: striped bass (rockfish), shad, and two species of herring. These fish are anadromous—they live in the oceans but ascend the rivers of the Atlantic Coast to spawn in the spring. The rockfish are considered semi-anadromous because they stay in the Bay for several years before going to sea. Pollution, overfishing, dams, and other stream blockages have drastically reduced the runs of all these fish, but they persist, and major efforts are underway to restore them on the Chesapeake.

The rockfish and shad stay in the rivers' main stems and are not readily apparent except to fishermen, but the herring create a lot of surface commotion. In late April, the species doing the spawning is the alewife, or "river herring" (not to be confused with the menhaden, which is sometimes called alewife). In May, the alewife run ends, and the adults return to the ocean, but they are replaced by the slightly smaller blueback herring. During the runs, many people dip herring from small headwater streams and put them up for everything from crab bait to people food. Salt roe herring and batterbread is a staple Sunday breakfast in Virginia.

Shad and herring are plankton feeders throughout their lives. Adult rockfish are omnivorous, but the larvae and early juveniles feed on plankton too. The spring copepod bloom has obvious value for their young, who stay behind in the rivers and creeks for the summer, mixing with the young of perch, pickerel, bass, and other locals.

Unlike fish, birds are warm-blooded, and those that winter on the Bay have been active all through that season. As the days lengthen and the rivers warm up, waterfowl begin to grow restive, and several species begin to show some mating behavior. By mid-March, most of them leave, migrating northward. The tundra swans are in this group, and many Canada geese leave during March as well.

Perhaps the finest moment in mid-March occurs when the ospreys return from South America. They come back to use the same nests year after year, and an individual pair of birds will usually return within two or three days of the same date they arrived the year before. They rest briefly from their trip and then begin to repair the nest in preparation for breeding and raising their young.

The ospreys' relatives, the bald eagles, began nesting in January, so early spring finds them rearing young. The adults can be seen fishing and soaring over the rivers, but the nests are purposely isolated, so they may be hard to find.

In April, spotted sandpipers appear along the rivers. These small brown-backed birds pick along the shoreline, especially at low tide, looking for worms, small snails, and other invertebrates. They look like many other sandpipers, but they bob their tails up and down, a characteristic of their species that helps to identify them. They are on their way from wintering grounds in Central and South America to breeding grounds on the Arctic tundra. For about a month there will be a few of them resting and feeding on each river in the Bay system.

By mid-April, many of the tidal fresh marsh plants are beginning to show themselves. Arrow arum and pickerelweed shoots come up and are recognizable almost immediately, dotting the shoreline here and there. Behind them, on the high marsh, tiny shoots of grass begin to appear on the bare mud. They look at first like extra-delicate field grass, but anyone who has watched the marshes from year to year knows them to be wild rice. These early shoots are much less impressive than the plant's later stages. They will grow to a height of eight or nine feet by August, but for now, as they develop, their brilliant soft green color offers an attractive contrast to the deeper, glossier green of the arrow arum and pickerelweed. Creeks with steep banks will be showing off white blossoms from shadbush, wild cherry trees, and wild plums, and pink blossoms from wild azalea at the same time.

By late May, the bulrushes are up, and the undergrowth of smartweed and tearthumb has begun. The steep banks will be showing off more blossoms from laurel bushes, and the sweetbay magnolia trees that line the creeks will be putting out fragrant white blossoms of their own.

Brackish Rivers—Farther downriver, in the brackish areas, things happen more slowly. Fish like menhaden and spot that were around until late in the fall headed out of the Bay to the continental shelf for the winter, leaving only the completely estuarine species behind. These include white perch, killifish, silversides, anchovies, and hogchokers. As spring comes to brackish waters, the perch move to lower salinity areas to spawn, as noted above. The other fish begin to move to shallower waters, also preparing to spawn. Male crabs that have overwintered up the rivers in the mud begin to stir themselves too.

Otters, coons, and muskrats, having been active in all but extreme winter weather, continue to busy themselves around. Pickings for these animals is still slim until late March, but then their food bases expand considerably, and the animals eat heartily. The brackish waters too have their ospreys, and their return is a real promise of warmer weather to come.

Another high point comes in April, when the first juvenile spot begin to show in the shallows. Spot spawn on the continental shelf in January, and larvae are swept up into the Bay shortly thereafter. The deep current on the Bay bottom carries them upstream, upriver, and up the main stem of the Bay in huge numbers. With even a rudimentary understanding of the Chesapeake's two-layered flow, it is easy enough to see how this kind of thing happens, but it still seems like a miracle of spring to stand on the bank well up the Rappahannock or the Wye or even the Patapsco, sort through a seine net catch, and find an inch-long spot there. This old behavior pattern, which the species has been practicing for a long time, ensures that these fish get an opportunity to feed in the rich nursery areas of the brackish rivers and salt marshes. Those that survive the summer will leave in the fall, having grown from a length of one inch to well over five inches.

Juvenile menhaden follow the same basic pattern, though they generally don't show up in the rivers in large numbers until May. Like the spot, they will be around all summer.

Also by mid-May, crabs will have started to move in the main Bay and the lower ends of most of the tributaries. Soft crabbers generally figure that the first big run of peelers shedding their shells comes in mid-May on the new moon or the full moon. It's a reliable piece of folk wisdom around Crisfield, Smith Island, and Tangier that this run coincides with the blooming of the locust trees on land.

Young crabs also begin to appear. All the Chesapeake's blue crabs are hatched near its mouth. Tiny juveniles are another gift to the rivers from the two-layered escalator currents.

As the shallows warm, the fish communities in the coves receive juvenile spot, menhaden, and crabs, as noted, plus anchovies and silversides that have wintered in deeper water. They join the killifish and grass shrimp that have been there all winter. There are not many predators in these nurseries, which is good for all the young.

The few predators that do frequent the coves prosper too. White perch gorge on shrimp. Otters catch plenty of fish at night. The most obvious fishermen are the great blue herons, which have been living on thin rations since October. They take advantage of the newly abundant food until April, when the adults head for their isolated rookeries to breed, nest, and raise the year's young.

Salt Marshes—In late March and early April, the open Bay is still cold, and although water temperatures are rising at the southern end, there is not a lot of obvious activity. Still, things are happening. Rockfish are headed up the Bay to their spawning grounds. So are the shad and herring. Those of us in small boats won't see them, but they are the first spring miracle for the pound net fishermen of the lower Bay. (Read "Spring" in *Beautiful Swimmers* for a good description.)

One of the best sights of early spring on the open Bay is the loons getting ready to migrate to north country lakes. They change from their simple brown-and-white winter plumage to their striking black-and-white summer plumage in March. (In transition, they can look mighty strange!) They feed actively on the arriving herring and menhaden to store up energy for their journey.

Spring is a time for migration, and the open Bay is a major corridor for water birds like cormorants and grebes, as well as ducks, geese, and swans. If your favorite saltmarsh has a beach to walk, walk it, and scan the open waters with your binoculars. Be sure to take a field guide. You'll see some birds that surprise you.

By mid-April, fish that have wintered on the continental shelf begin to enter the Chesapeake. Second- and third-year-class menhaden come first. Behind them, and feeding voraciously on them, come bluefish up to twenty pounds. The largest of the fish will stay in the Bay for a month or so. When the water temperature gets up over 70°F, they leave either by the Chesapeake and Delaware Canal at the head of the Bay or by turning around and swimming back down and out through the Virginia Capes. The smaller fish, those under ten pounds, enter in waves beginning in June and are around till fall.

In the salt marshes, the waterfowl leave in March and the ospreys return. Small killifish begin to stir themselves in marsh pools. Still, nothing much happens until the estuarine fish move in April or May, first the juvenile spot, then the menhaden, and then gradually young trout, mullet, flounder, and others. Green growth begins on the cordgrasses in April and continues. Shorebirds like willits and oystercatchers begin nesting, and they complain loudly at any intrusion on their territory. Because these saltmarsh areas are close to large expanses of water, the temperatures in all but the shallowest change relatively slowly. By mid-May, however, spring is moving in in full force. The crabs shed, fish roam the shallows, ospreys hunt for food for their newly hatched chicks, and great blue herons head off to their rookeries.

Early spring is an acquired taste. The weather can be as rotten then as at any other time, but when it breaks, the feeling is glorious. Remember that spring comes in pieces. Its progress is not always obvious, but a great deal is happening. Later on, in April and May, spring does show itself in full flower. Watching the details of change in the season is one of those things that is all too easy to forget in the press of modern life. To the careful observer, however, it is a whole string of miracles. The world starts up anew, and the adventurous small boat explorer is there to be a part of it.

Summer

Summer is a good time to be on the Bay. No matter how much we appreciate the other seasons, this is when we seem to have the most time to spend on the water.

For the small boat explorer, summer can mean paddling up a tidal fresh creek surrounded by lush greenery and marsh flowers in bloom, or stalking soft crabs with a roller net in a brackish creek, or walking a secluded beach at the edge of a big salt marsh. There is a lot to see and do.

Be careful out there, though. Days are usually hot and humid, and there is nearly always a chance of an afternoon thunderstorm. For a number of reasons, this is a good season for getting an early start on a day's exploring. The sun is less glaring on the water, protection from it is less of a problem, and the chance of encountering a thunderstorm is minimized.

Tidal Fresh Rivers—The Chesapeake Bay Foundation has been running its two-week summer field trips for the Maryland State Department of Education for well over fifteen years, but I can still remember the fascination with which those of us involved with the first series of trips in 1977 watched the progression of development of the tidal fresh marshes on the Patuxent River. It was the first chance that any of us had had to examine a specific tidal fresh marsh community on a regular basis, every two to three weeks, through the entire summer. We were even more excited than the students. Despite the heat, we couldn't wait to get up Mattaponi and Terrapin creeks to see what was growing. The profusion of greenery at first, and then of flowers and seeds, staggered our imaginations. On the first trip, in June, we made our way up Terrapin Creek to its fresher waters past walls of giant cordgrass and cattails interspersed with buttonbush. At the head of the creek we found almost junglelike greenery, with arrow arum and pickerelweed at the water's edge. Behind these floating-leaved plants, on the muddy surface of the marsh itself, grew water dock, smartweed, tearthumb, wild rice, tidemarsh waterhemp, hibiscus, rice cutgrass, and narrow-leaved cattail. There were as many shades and textures of green as there were species of plants.

In early July, a new color appeared. The orange parasitic vine dodder took off like wildfire, wrapping itself especially around the arrow arum and smartweed. Having never seen it before, we worried about it. By late July, it had blazed trails across the marsh, leaving wilted plants behind it. But as dodder kills its host plants, it kills itself as well, and by early August, new shoots of arrow arum had begun to grow up in its wake. We realized just how resilient these plant communities are.

To our delight, flowers appeared in July. The first were the blue fingers of the pickerelweed. By late July, a few crimson-centered hibiscus flowers had begun to show. By early August, the white flowers and seeds of smartweed had come out, along with the pink seeds of its relative, tearthumb. The waterhemp was well on its way to producing a heavy crop of seeds, and the wild rice flowers had come out, pale yellow promises of rich grains to come. At the head of the creek, rice cutgrass had begun to put up its seeds. Perhaps most spectacular of all, at least in terms of numbers, the arrow arum seedpods had swelled into large green bulbs, which popped open to yield large numbers of thumbnail-sized

A tidal fresh marsh on the Chester River, bursting with life in the summer.

brown seeds which we would be seeing along the river banks of all the tidal rivers for the next three or four months.

As we dug into our field guides, we began to realize what a tremendous crop of wildlife food was being produced right there in the marsh for the waterfowl that would be coming in the fall. The arrow arum seeds hold a great deal of oxalic acid, which prevents most birds from feeding on them, but wood ducks apparently can stand the hot taste and relish the seeds, which have excellent nutritional value. Rice cutgrass has excellent food value, as does Walter's millet, a grass that went unnoticed in the marshes until its wheatlike seed heads came out in August.

It was perhaps easiest to relate to the wild rice, whose grains are noted for both their taste and their nutritional value. Rice is extremely important to migratory waterfowl as they come out of their summering grounds in central Canada. They stop off in Minnesota and Wisconsin, feeding heavily on rice in that area in September. Our rice is ripe about the same time, but there are only a few waterfowl here then. These few teal and wood ducks gorge on it, as do red-winged blackbirds and bobolinks. By the time the other ducks get down to the Chesapeake, most of the rice has either been eaten by these early birds or has sunk into the marsh to make more rice for the next year.

The primary duck food producers are instead smartweed and tearthumb, two relatives of buckwheat that produce tons of nutritious seeds in late August and early September. Their white and pink seeds add even more color to the late summer marshes. Tearthumb, by the way, is so named because of its scratchy stem. It is the plant that taught us to wear long pants in the marshes.

The creeks in August, then, produce a smorgasbord for seed-eating wildlife. It is well worth the hot work of paddling up them to watch this botanical drama unfold and to realize what it means for the system.

The other aspect of those trips that facinated us was the diversity of fishlife that came up in the minnow seine when we pulled it. It was common to catch fifteen different species at a time. The mixture was astounding. There were always spottail shiners, sunfish, young chain pickerel, largemouth bass, and other freshwater fish. We routinely caught estuarine species like anchovies, silversides, white perch, and juvenile rockfish. There were usually some grass shrimp as well. Finally, there would always be a few species that had come from 'way down the Bay or even out on the continental shelf, especially juvenile crabs, spot, and menhaden.

The distribution of menhaden is always particularly remarkable. Every nook and cranny of every tidal fresh, brackish, and salty river or creek seems to have young-of-the-year menhaden in it in the summertime. The total number of them in the Bay system must have an awful lot of zeros in it.

As we watched through other summers, we began to see patterns of plant distribution in wet and dry years. Dry years seem particularly to favor the waterhemp. I watched one individual plant grow to a height of thirteen feet on Terrapin Creek in 1978. By September, when the plant died, the base of its trunk was a full six inches in diameter. It looked like a young cedar tree. Not bad for three months' growth from an annual plant. Wet years seemed to favor wild rice, and these summers tended to cut down on the number of crabs and spot in the seine, though the menhaden always seemed to be as abundant as ever.

As the summer program grew, we began to explore other rivers in both Maryland and Virginia on a regular basis, and of course we found the same patterns of marsh development in all those other areas as well. It is hot work poking up a narrow marsh creek in July, and the water is usually over 80°F (26.7°C), so there is not a great deal of relief to be gained by getting into it. The rewards, however, are in what one sees. Summer is a great time to learn Chesapeake Bay botany and to begin to develop an understanding of the essential role that the Bay's marsh plants play in the way the whole system works.

Brackish Rivers—Summer is crab time in the Chesapeake's brackish rivers, creeks, and coves. Blue crabs do some of their best growing in midrange salinities, so the finest crab-growing habitat in the Bay system is in these areas. The Wye River, for example is generally considered to be the prime producer of No. 1 jimmy crabs. At the same time, these areas provide prime growing habitat for young crabs as well. Thus all sizes turn up in the brackish rivers in the summer. There is abundant food available for them, and the modest rebound in submerged grasses like widgeongrass and horned pondweed in the past several years has provided good shedding habitat where soft crabs can hide until their new shells harden.

It is always satisfying for someone who wants a meal of steamed crabs to net a number of big crabs from baited lines or trotlines. Likewise, it is always satisfying to hunt the grass beds around the time of the new moon or the full moon and pick up soft crabs, but the real time of wonder comes simply in watching juvenile crabs swim around in these nursery areas, or in walking the bank and finding good numbers of sloughs (discarded shells) from young crabs that are growing rapidly. It is well to remember that these young crabs, no matter in what brackish river we find them, have come from spawning areas in the lower Bay and have traveled briefly out onto the continental shelf, as far as forty miles into the Atlantic, before being swept back into the Bay. The full travels of our Bay's crabs during their life cycle are only just now being understood. As is the case with juvenile spot (see "Spring"), it is a miracle of the Chesapeake's hydraulic machinery that juvenile crabs an inch across the shell can be found in tributaries as far up the Bay as the Chester on the Eastern Shore, or the Bush on the western shore, or up into the Rappahannock to Port Royal and beyond. They are major figures in the brackish river systems, providing food at once to creatures as diverse as man, otters, white perch, and great blue herons, while they in turn perform valuable roles as scavengers.

Another scavenger, whose role is much more commonly overlooked, is the grass shrimp. These little crustaceans reach a maximum size of two inches. They occur at almost all salinities, from nearly fresh to nearly seawater, so they are widely distributed throughout the Bay. As their name implies, they flourish in grass beds, but they are common also around almost any kind of wooden cover, from dock pilings and bulkheads to fallen trees. There are thousands of tons of them in the Bay system.

Grass shrimp are not normally eaten by humans, though their flavor is good if they are steamed. Pinch off the heads and eat the tails whole. They are most important, however, as fish food. Because of their wide distribution, they are eaten by species as diverse as sunfish and largemouth bass up the rivers and by trout and flounder down near the Bay's mouth. Two species whose broad distribution in the Bay system parallels that of the grass shrimp and which thus are major predators on it are the white perch and its first cousin, the rockfish (striped bass).

Catching and caring for grass shrimp in warm weather could be the subject of a chapter in itself. Suffice it to say that pushing a dip net or a roller net with very fine mesh through grass beds or along old dock pilings will yield enough bait for a morning of serious fishing, and the shrimp will keep well for an hour or two early and late in the day in a bucket half-filled with river water. In truly hot conditions, keep them on screen-bottomed racks in an ice chest, cool but away from the ice water at the bottom.

Another major figure in the brackish rivers at this time of year is the great blue heron. By midsummer, most of the adults have fledged their young and moved from the isolated rookeries back to their home rivers, creeks, and coves. Although they are distributed throughout the system, many stake their claims on the brackish portions of the rivers, because there is so much life in them in the summertime. The heron's diet in these areas consists of small crabs, juvenile menhaden, silversides, anchovies, killifish, and sometimes even grass shrimp. Watching the birds stalk the shallows is one of the best parts of being on the river.

A relative of the great blue heron that is also active but less obvious is the little green heron. It is a much smaller bird, with legs altogether too short for wading. Little green herons take advantage of the abundance of fallen trees along the shores of many of the creeks and coves, using branches at the water level as ambush points for small fish that congregate around and take refuge in the branches. Here the birds' small size works to their advantage, for their strike is faster than that of their much taller relatives, and they can fish areas that are too deep for even great blue herons to wade.

Green herons have an uncanny knack of moving from branch to branch on fallen trees. It is easy enough to miss one, till startled by the sudden presence of a human being in a small boat, it gives out its raucous warning squawk (on the middle Eastern Shore, they are known as "skouks" because of the cry) and fly off to another tree. Once you get used to spotting them, look closely. They are beautiful birds, with iridescent green backs and chestnut brown breasts streaked with white.

Another member of the brackish river community whose antics are worth watching in summer is the belted kingfisher. Like the herons, these birds feed on small fish in the rivers, but they do so by diving. Their aim is accurate, and their movements are quick. Like ospreys, they come up from the water with their quarry, shake in midair, and fly off to their perches.

Like the little green heron, they resent intrusions and chatter loudly at human beings who invade their territories. They also are very aggressive towards other kingfishers who come into those territories. Follow one up a creek, and it will fly only to the edge of its own territory, doubling back through the woods when it reaches the boundary rather than incurring the wrath of its neighbor. As you watch a kingfisher work its water, think about how its way of life is different enough from those of herons and ospreys that all these fishing birds can coexist. There is plenty to mull over on that subject.

Salt Marshes—Early summer produces a feast of greens in the salt marshes. The cordgrasses and other plants are reaching their peak of growth, and every particle of usable soil will be occupied.

Saltmarsh bulrush will have flowered in late spring, so its large brown seed heads will be formed by early summer. This three-sided sedge grows in low spots on the high marsh, and it will form its deeper green against the lush bright green of the saltmeadow hay.

The meadows themselves will appear to be a thick thatch. Much of the marsh in these areas is firm and good for walking, so by all means take a walk around, but look carefully as you go. There are small holes and muskrat leads that form soft places which can swallow a leg in the blink of an eye. Test your weight always before putting your foot down hard. Saltmeadow hay and its companion meadow plant, saltgrass, both will flower and form their seeds around midsummer.

Meanwhile, saltmarsh cordgrass will be growing in the lower tidal areas and the edges of the marsh guts. This plant will be taller than the saltmeadow hay, although on the back edges of the stands, there may be a band of shorter individuals. These plants are on flats that are flooded less regularly than the soils of the creek banks but more frequently than the once- or twice-a-month storm tide regimen that best suits salt-meadow hay. Most plants of the short form saltmarsh cordgrass will not flower and make seeds, but the tall form that grows along the banks of the guts will be flowering and making its seeds during August.

Saltmarsh fleabane, a relative of camphor, puts out its purple flower in July to add a touch of color. By late July, the pink seashore mallows will be beginning to bloom, as will the crimson-centered white or pink marsh hibiscus.

By mid-August, the cordgrass will be beginning to develop a tinge of gold. This is actually a sign of fall—the above-ground sections of these perennial plants are beginning to die. Their death, however, will be slow, and in the meantime they will add a golden tint to the collection of greens and pinks and whites of the saltmarshes. The marsh elder will flower in the most inconspicuous fashion, and suddenly in August the observer will discover that the plant has developed heads of small green berries. Groundsel tree, the other saltbush, will still be developing its flowers. They will be among the last to appear, early in the fall.

Summer salt marshes, then, are mostly great expanses of green against a hazy summer sky. Birds around them will tend to be less noticeable than in June. The willits and oystercatchers will have finished their nesting and will be less demonstrative in defense of their territories.

In fact, by the latter part of July, many of them will have already begun their migration south. The herons and the egrets will all be active, again primarily at dawn and dusk.

Ospreys will be busy all day. During the first half of the summer, they are feeding their young, which grow at such an astounding rate that by late July, at the age of two months, they are nearly as large as their parents. There will be much activity around their nests until then. By late July, the young will have fledged (learned to fly). Then begins a period of learning to fish. They and their parents will increasingly be away from the nest, but they will still be much in evidence around the waterways for the rest of the summer. By early September, most of them will be leaving for their wintering grounds in Central and South America.

On the marshes themselves, perhaps the most active birds are the red-winged blackbirds and long-billed marsh wrens. These animals are seed eaters. The staples of their diets are the seeds that grow from the bulrushes, the cordgrasses, and the other marsh plants. Laughing gulls and terns will be feeding in the marsh guts, concentrating primarily on small fish. Other water birds will turn up for the enterprising explorer who keeps eyes and ears open.

Mammals in the salt marshes are active also in summer. It is a season when food is abundant for them and therefore often a time when they are feeding young. Again, however, they are active primarily at dawn and dusk or at night. As always, it pays to learn to read animal tracks and scats. Visit a saltmarsh cove early on a summer morning and you will find that the neighborhood otters, coons, and muskrats all have been crisscrossing each others' trails during the night.

In the water, there is a great deal of growing going on. The perennial of the saltmarsh guts, the killifishes, seem to be active all the time. A push with a roller net through the water at the edge of the marsh bank may turn up individuals that vary in length from half an inch to six inches. At times when the tide is running strong in the guts, fish may boil on the surface like miniature rockfish feeding.

They and their cousins, the sheepshead minnows, live also in the salt pannes, the shallow pools on the surfaces of the marsh meadows. The pannes are perhaps the salt marshes' most rigorous environment: temperatures go well over 100°F (37.8°C), while oxygen drops and salinity rises to more than that of seawater. No matter—the killifish can adapt to these conditions, and as they do, they find abundant food in the pools. Anchovies and silversides likewise are active in the salt marshes in the summertime, but not in the pannes.

Sentinel in the marsh, the ubiquitous male red-winged blackbird. Photo by Bill Portlock.

Perhaps the most striking example of growth over the course of a summer comes with observation of the juvenile spot. When they reach the salt marshes in April, each one is less than an inch long, as noted in the "Spring" section. These young of the year must feed incessantly. Early on, they find large numbers of tiny sea worms and crustaceans like amphipods. They continue to feed on these as they grow, but they add to their diet barnacles, anemones, and other creatures that they can nibble from the bottom. The variety of food available to them increases. By the time they leave the marshes in the fall, many are over four inches.

Young-of-the-year menhaden likewise will more than double their length over the course of the summer. They graze incessantly on the plankton communities available to them. The water surface of a salt marsh gut at any time may display four or five cat's-paws, each of which is caused by anywhere from several hundred to a thousand small fish busily gulping their way through fertile plankton blooms.

A number of fish species use these marsh guts as nurseries, though the sheer bulk of their numbers may be smaller than those of the commonest species. When pulling a minnow seine, there is always a temptation to say "Ho hum, more killifish, silversides, spot, and menhaden." Don't let yourself become too blasé. These fish represent the basic economy of the system and therefore are worth watching because they are so fundamental to the way it operates. It is, however, always worthwhile to keep an eye peeled for the unusual. In poking through the salt marshes with a cast net, we come occasionally upon juvenile gray trout and speckled trout, as well as young red drum and even rare species that seem to be out of their ranges, like groupers. Pay attention at first to the basic fish in the area, but once you have learned your way around, it is definitely valuable to carry a detailed field guide to identify unusual individuals.

Fall

It's four o'clock in the afternoon on a Wednesday in mid-October. The sky is bell clear, and the nip in the air makes a sweater feel good over a flannel shirt. The canoes are all loaded on the trailer. A schoolbus full of excited but tired seventh-graders has just left. Suddenly it is quiet; for the first time since morning, all I can hear are river sounds: geese flying, red-winged blackbirds foraging for the last of the wild rice in the marsh across the way, the tide gurgling around the dock at the launch point. I sit on the bank, a mug of tea in hand, and unwind.

The river in this particular scene is the Patuxent at Jug Bay, but it could as easily be Totuskey Creek on the Rappahannock, or Kings Creek on the Choptank, or the Mattaponi at Walkerton, or a host of others. Fall is a wonderful time to be out.

This is a paradoxical season. It is a rich time, when the promises of spring and summer are fulfilled. Plants have reached their peak growth. Annuals like wild rice and smartweed have produced heavy crops of seeds. Perennials like saltmarsh cordgrass are thick and tall. Fish from white perch to bluefish are in prime condition, fat from feeding heavily on summer's bounty.

Even so, the crisp air promises the bleakness of winter. The cordgrass leaves may be tall, but they are turning gold, on the way to dying. The rice is brown and falling over. The fish are getting fat to tide them through lean times in cold water.

All the Bay's creatures are getting ready for winter. The cordgrass leaves, through the process of photosynthesis, have turned the energy of sunlight into starch in the plant's rootstocks. This stored energy will carry the plant through the winter and help it put out new leaves in the spring. The rice has a different strategy, storing its energy in tons of seeds to grow whole new rice plants in the spring.

The perch will hole up in deep water for the winter, feeding only sporadically. The fat they build up in the fall will help them develop roe and milt to spawn next spring. The bluefish feed now on thick schools of menhaden before they migrate back to the ocean for winter.

Birds are busy migrating. Some, like ospreys and egrets, are headed south. Others, like Canada geese and ducks, are headed into the Bay from colder areas to the north.

Fall signals that the year is winding down, but it is too rich to allow us to dwell on pessimism. It is a long season, lasting in most years from the first cold front after Labor Day all the way to Christmas. It is a golden season, with lots to see and do. For anyone accustomed to thinking of the Bay as a summer plaything, fall is a revelation.

Tidal Fresh Rivers—In the upriver marshes, vegetation is still thick in the fall. The many dying leaves produce a mixture of colors and textures. Marsh hibiscus plants have dried up to brown stems and seedpods that earn the species the nickname "rattleweed," making it hard to remember the summer's showy blossoms. The last flower to bloom, tickseed sunflower, more than makes up for the difference. It spreads a bright carpet of yellow over the high marsh until frost. On the Patuxent, the plant is called "butterweed," a term of affection for its color and for the fat seeds that will offer waterfowl a nutritious late-winter food. Butterweed is the primary bloom, but there are other surprises. It's a good game, for example, to look for pickerelweed flowers in early October. There is always at least one. Some wild rice always blooms late on banks with southern exposure. Bill Portlock and I have seen it that way in mid-November down on the Chickahominy.

Tree colors form a good backdrop to the textures of the marshes. Red maples and ashes growing on wet ground contrast with the oaks of the high banks. There is often a backdrop of green on the latter, from hollies and laurel.

Several tidal fresh rivers have stands of cypress trees. Most notable are the Chickahominy, the Pocomoke, and Dragon Run (the head of the Piankatank). Isolated stands occur on the Patuxent (Battle Creek), the Nanticoke (Broad Creek), the Pamunkey, and the James. These trees are especially beautiful in the fall, when they turn a soft russet heather mixture of colors that mixes well on overcast days with the maples and ashes around them.

As noted, fall brings a rich crop of mast from the marshes and the trees. Stalks of Walters millet bend over with the weight of their grain. The seeds are distinctive. Each has a short and a long spike. Pick some from a plant and take a good look at them. Then look for others floating in the water. Now you understand why surface-feeding ducks like mallards, blacks, and teal spend so much time poking around in creek backwaters and marsh guts. Start looking at the surface scum in those areas, and you're at the heart of the reason why tidal fresh marshes are such good waterfowl habitat. Look at other seeds, like smartweed and tearthumb, while they are still on the plants, and then look for them on the water too.

Birds are an important part of fall in the upper rivers. At this time of year, it is helpful to think of them in four general groups: those that are migrating in for the winter, those that are leaving to go south, those that pass through going south, and those that stay year-round.

Waterfowl are the obvious newcomers. In early September, teal (both blue-winged and green-winged) start appearing in the rice marshes. Though a few are local breeders, most have come from summer grounds as far north as Canada. A few will winter here. Many more will pass through on the way to wintering grounds from South Carolina through the Caribbean to Venezuela. Behind them will come other surface-feeding ducks: blacks, mallards, pintails, gadwalls.

Toward the end of September, a rainy low-pressure system often stalls over the Bay country for several days. It will be followed by a strong cold front with a blast of cool northwest winds from Canada. The rain is a time of anticipation, for seasoned marsh watchers know that the cold front will bring the first big flights of Canada geese in from Hudson Bay. They are wise enough to ride the strong northwest winds, and they are magnificent sights, honking noisily as they fly high in perfect V-formation before breaking ranks and dropping down to marshes and fields they recognize from previous years. By mid-October, many are settled into daily routines, flying up and down the rivers from nighttime resting areas on the water to daytime feeding spots in harvested cornfields.

As October gives way to November, other waterfowl appear, especially tundra swans and diving ducks like canvasbacks and scaup. Both groups spend time on tidal fresh rivers, but they are more common downstream in brackish water, so we'll deal with them there.

As waterfowl arrive, other birds prepare to leave. By early September, our ospreys have fledged their young, taught them to fish, and departed with them to Central and South America for summer in the southern hemisphere. A few ospreys from New England and the Canadian Maritime Provinces pass through during October and November.

There are subtle shifts in the seagull populations. Several species are present all the time, like ring-billed and herring gulls, but individual birds that summer here move south, while others of the same species that spent the summer farther north move in. Laughing gulls change from summer to winter plumage and most fly south, but a few linger. The number of great black-backed gulls builds up. More fly in to winter than leave.

Several shorebirds fly through the Bay country, linger a while, and move on. Snipe and sora rails are especially common in the tidal fresh marshes. Snipe are most obvious, flying from the marsh at the approach of a boat. Sora will call out their odd whinnying cry but will seldom fly unless startled by a loud noise.

There is an old tradition of hunting sora on the tidal fresh rivers, especially the Patuxent and the Chickahominy. For years, guides poled shallow-draft skiffs through the marshes with their clients aboard and slapped their poles on the water's surface to make the birds fly. The sora are still there, but hunting them has mostly died out.

Spotted sandpipers move through. Their numbers are never large in any one place, but they seem to be everywhere. There is a period of time from late September to early November when we see one or two every day, no matter where we are. As noted previously in the discussion on spring, the bird identifies itself by its distinctive behavior—it bobs its tail almost constantly as it picks its way along the river shore. As a boat approaches, it flies downstream a hundred yards or so and starts walking again.

Three fishing birds have been around all summer and will stay right on through fall into winter. The great blue heron will continue to stalk the shallows, roost in tall pines next to the water, and fly away with a loud squawk as a boat approaches. Its cousin, the little green heron, will do well by perching on fallen trees and ambushing fish that swim by. The schools of young menhaden that hang around till frost are especially valuable to it. Finally, and perhaps most obvious because of its noisy chattering, the kingfisher will still dive on small fish that it spots from its perches in riverside trees.

The presence of these last three birds indicates the continued presence of fish. Juvenile menhaden, as noted, stay around most of the fall before heading back to the ocean. They and the ever-present killifish are still the mainstays of the fishing birds' diets. As the shallow waters cool, other forage fish like anchovies and shiners spend more of their time in deeper water.

Largemouth bass and chain pickerel divide their time between the shallows and the channel edges, feeding heavily to store up fat for the winter. Fall is an active time for them. Channel catfish tend to stay in the deeper waters, but they too are active. Smaller predators like white perch, yellow perch, and crappie are feeding too, especially around fallen trees along the banks. "Fishing the wood" is a good strategy for anglers pursuing these three species and bass too.

Brackish Rivers—Cordgrasses turn gold in the fall sun. The plants are perennials, dying back to their root systems in the fall after their growth has peaked and their seeds have formed. As the green of the leaves fades to gold, the combination is striking, especially in afternoon light.

Several other marsh plants enhance the effect. One of the saltbushes, groundsel tree, flowers in September and then produces its seeds in hundreds of little tufts of white that last into November. Seaside goldenrod blooms, and so does the saltmarsh aster. The result is splashes of white and yellow mixed into the green and gold of the cordgrasses.

In the creeks, the fall colors of the trees enhance the effect. The mixture is different from the tidal fresh rivers but still attractive: sycamores, tulip poplars, white oaks, willow oaks, persimmons, and maples are set off by evergreen Virginia pines and red cedars. If the creek has high banks, red oaks, beech, laurel, and holly will add their colors and textures. Again, the best colors will show in indirect light, on overcast days or at dawn and dusk.

As the marshes die back, muskrat lodges become more apparent. While in summer the best evidence of the animals' presence has been chopped-off stems of cordgrass floating on the surface, now their houses of grass and sedge stalks stand out on the marsh. The animals are eating busily to store up fat for the winter, so they are digging into the mud for the starchy rhizomes that the plants have stored for their own use. Thus the marsh around each lodge is often eaten out, increasing the structure's visibility. The animals increase this effect because they pile up new stalks to insulate their lodges against the winter's cold.

The autumnal equinox brings extreme tides, both low and high. The lowest tides allow raccoons to hunt clams on shallow flats that are normally inaccessible to them. Between the tides, the coons busily gorge themselves on their favorite fall food: persimmons. While summertime coon droppings usually show a diet of crabs and mussels, in the fall they are full of big orange persimmon seeds.

The otters are busy now too. Even though they manage to fish all winter, there are more of both quantity and variety of prey available to them in October and November than there will be later on. Juvenile menhaden, spot, trout, and bluefish are favored foods, but those fish will leave with the first hard frost or snowfall. As usual, the otters make themselves as inconspicuous as possible, but the careful observer will still see them now and then, and the droppings on their trails will tell of their comings and goings.

As noted above, many of the fish in the brackish rivers leave for winter. Thus fall is a time for schooling up and feeding heavily before departing for the more stable temperatures of the continental shelf and the deepest holes in the rivers. In the biggest brackish river of all, the Bay itself, the charter boat fleet finds a bonanza of bluefish, trout, and flounder that sometimes lasts till mid-November. When legal, rockfish add to the excitement. This is big boat water, but the small boat explorer can find good fishing in the mouths of any of the big rivers, from the Chester down to the James. The city newspapers carry a running narrative of the action, from the first schooling-up to the migration southward and out through the Capes to the Atlantic.

As the menhaden build into large schools, bluefish feed heavily on them. One of the season's best attractions is casting surface lures to them as they drive the smaller fish to the surface to attack them. Fishing a

Taskinas Creek at the York River State Park—brackish at the mouth but tidal fresh in the two headwater tributaries. Photo by Bill Portlock.

school of breaking bluefish is exciting sport, with baitfish jumping, blues boiling behind them, gulls wheeling and diving into the melee, and anglers working to maneuver boats, cast, fight fish, and land them safely. This scene is a clear reminder that we are top-line predators.

Such fishing is exhilarating, and it can make an angler proud. But the Bay has lots of ways of putting us in our places too. One of my favorite ways to be humbled is to chase a breaking school and find out that it isn't fish at all, but loons. Off in the distance, seagulls gather in a cloud, wheeling and diving over panicky baitfish. The water boils as the predators attack from beneath. But get there and there aren't any big fish. Instead several loons pop up to the surface, looking satisfied with themselves.

They are remarkably powerful birds underwater. If the great blue heron is the master stalker and the osprey the most skilled at aerial attack, the loon is the champion diver for fish.

Our loons are the same ones we associate with northern lakes. Large numbers spend the fall here, in the rivers, and out in the open Bay. But look closely for them, because at this season they are in winter plumage: chestnut brown backs with white throats and breasts. Stand on the shore of most any brackish river in November, and you will see at least a couple of the birds alternately resting and diving.

At this season on some rivers, there will be flocks of cormorants. These are large diving birds with superficial resemblances to loons while on the water and to Canada geese while flying. They too are adept fishers.

Of course there will be geese too. Most of our birds have come down from their summer breeding grounds on the Ungava Peninsula, the eastern side of Hudson Bay in Canada. In a few rivers, especially on the Eastern Shore, there may be some snow geese as well. By mid-November, there will be tundra swans. These great white birds come to us from summer grounds on the tundra of the Arctic Coast and the Bering Straits. On the way down, they stop for an extended rest in the prairie potholes of North Dakota before arriving here. It's a good trick to learn by ear the difference between a flock of swans flying overhead and a flock of geese. The swans' calls seem to be higher-pitched and quavering instead of the sturdy honks of the geese. Listen carefully and watch closely. You'll learn.

Various other migratory waterfowl appear on the brackish rivers, most after the first of November. With all of these birds potentially out on the water, a good way to look is to stand on the bank and scan the river with a pair of binoculars. Begin by looking as far upstream as you can and swing slowly down till you are looking directly across. Then swing slowly downstream. At first, it feels like staring off into space, but you will be surprised how much you see this way.

One final note. By mid-fall, most of the phytoplankton in the brackish rivers has died off, and the water is clear. This is a great time for ghosting along in the shallows with a canoe. It feels like floating in space. Be sure to look over the side. All sorts of things will turn up in the water below you.

Salt Marshes—Much of what has been said about brackish rivers applies to the salt marshes. The cordgrasses turn gold, backed by blooming seaside goldenrod and groundsel tree. Geese, swans, and loons all appear. Most of the fish leave for deeper water or for the ocean. Muskrat lodges will suddenly stand out on the open marsh. The scene can be stark, but it is often beautiful. This is a great season for beachcombing.

Raccoons will be active, but their foods will differ a bit from those of their upriver brethren. If persimmons are available in the scrub woods be- hind the marsh, they will of course hunt for them. And the equinoctial low tides will allow them to forage the shallows more widely than usual. They will find there a greater variety of shellfish than is available upriver, and they will feed heavily on the ribbed mussels they find growing in the marsh banks.

Otters too will remain active, feeding on young menhaden, spot, and trout till those species leave, then shifting to killifish. These hardy little fish will stay all year, and they are amazingly adaptable. They eat whatever is available, from insect larvae in warm weather to decayed plant material in cold. In fall and winter, they are most active in sun-warmed shallows. In colder conditions, they bury themselves in the mud.

Saltmarsh coves are great places to look for sea ducks like oldsquaws and scoters, as well as bay ducks like goldeneye, canvasbacks, and scaup. Again, stand on the shore and scan the water with binoculars. Some of these divers will raft up, while others are scattered in ones and twos. They may be resting or feeding on the rich benthic communities below them.

A Note about Cold Weather—As the weather gets colder, cold-blooded vertebrates like fish and turtles slow down. Some become dormant, as do invertebrates like crabs. Oysters, worms, and other bottom dwellers continue their limited activities, but at reduced rates. Only warm-blooded animals like birds and mammals continue their activities, and all of them have special behavioral or structural adaptations to help them maintain their body temperatures.

It is useful at this time to remember that we are mammals who deal with cold weather by changing our behavior, especially by adding heat-trapping structures like sweaters and jackets. In late fall and winter, the small boat explorer does well to be *very* conservative about weather and to confine cruises to sheltered bodies of water. Keep your boat and gear in top shape.

Be especially careful about getting wet, and carry extra clothes in a waterproof bag in case something happens. Hypothermia is a sneaky killer. Be wary of it. Taking care of yourself will help you stay comfortable and relaxed, so you'll notice more of your surroundings. Enjoy your cold weather time on the water.

Winter

The day was chilly, but the wind was still, the sky was clear, and the January sun did what it could to melt the patchy skim ice on the Severn River. I pushed the canoe out into the water, and Marshyhope jumped into the boat, her tail wagging. On days when the water temperature is below 40°F and the river can suck all the heat out of the legs of anybody who walks in hip boots, it is amazing to watch a dog bounding around with no apparent discomfort.

Marshyhope jumped back out of the boat and trotted down the shore while I poled along behind her. Two hundred yards away from our launch, she stopped and began sniffing the beach intently. When I got close enough to look, the story was plain. Fresh raccoon tracks were all over the narrow beach, but a short trail of them ran out fifty feet into the river, ending in a shallow bottom crater about three feet in diameter.

The moon had been full the night before, producing a very low tide. The water was very near to 39.1°F (4°C), the temperature at which it is densest. Thus the river had actually shrunk in volume as winter had come. A passing cold front the day before had brought twenty-five-knot winds from the northwest, pushing the water out of the river. The three factors together had produced abnormally low water about dawn that morning, and the raccoon had known how to make the most of the opportunity.

This stretch of shoreline has a healthy population of *Macoma balthica*, a small, thin-shelled clam which has no commercial value (to us) but which is superb and important wildlife food—for any animal with access to it. The coon had foraged the shallows and thinned out the population there earlier in the winter. Now the tide offered it a chance to work on some new territory usually available only to the canvasbacks, buffleheads, and other diving ducks wintering on the river. Unlike

Marshyhope, who could go back indoors and lie in front of a fire to dry out and warm up, the coon preferred not to get very wet. It was living on a fine line between the need to hunt food and the need to keep from lowering its body temperature unnecessarily.

Marshyhope and I worked our way back into a nearby tidal pond, and I pushed the boat into the edge of a small pocket marsh. Normally the ravine that feeds it is choked with brambles and poison ivy, but not now. Winter's bleakness can be an asset sometimes. We walked up. From the hillside, we could look down into the creek bottom, and there, in the crook of a big gum tree's trunk, was our coon. It was asleep, curled up in the sun, soaking up the warmth, contented with what may have been its first full stomach in a couple of weeks. I wish that I could say my dog and I were stealthy as Indians, but we weren't. The coon woke up and turned its head in our direction, but it was far out of our reach and knew it, so it went back to sleep. I was familiar with the tree and knew there was a hollow in the base of its trunk. In extreme weather, the coon could use the hollow, and it might even sleep there for a week at a time. Raccoons sleep by day and forage at night. We had found this animal in its bed.

Warm-blooded animals are the most active and obvious members of the Bay's winter community. Ducks, geese, and swans are still around. Although hunting seasons are over, anyone who enjoys the birds can find a few good winter days watching them afield. Herons and gulls scratch out meager livings, as do raccoons, muskrats, and river otters. The otters, in fact, seem to be more visible now than at any other time of year. Normally secretive, they play enthusiastically during daylight hours, even in creeks with docks and marinas. They seem to know that they enjoy February more than most of the Bay's other animals do.

Winter temperatures force most of the Bay's creatures into inactivity or dormancy. Cold-blooded animals, whose body temperatures are basically dependent on that of their environment, are most susceptible to the season. As water temperatures drop in late fall and early winter, they seek out the warmest habitats they can find where temperatures are stable. In general, the most comfortable place to be is in deep water.

Water has several physical properties which enhance the value of deep holes as winter habitat. First is the property of reaching maximum density at 39.1°F (4°C). As it cools beyond that point, it gets less dense, which is why ice floats. Subfreezing air temperatures will cause surface waters to cool to 32°F (0°C) and then freeze, but bottom waters will remain around 4°C.

The second important property of water, also discussed in "Spring," is its high specific heat. That is, it must absorb or lose large quantities of heat to change temperature. The greater the volume of water involved, the slower the change. In a prolonged cold snap, thick ice will form at the surface, but bottom waters will remain warm, especially in depths over ten feet or so. By contrast, shallow flats warm up rapidly by day but cool quickly at night. Deep holes remain the same, changing only slowly with the seasons.

Finally, cold water can hold gasses in solution at higher concentrations than can warm water. This property means that oxygen concentrations are higher in winter than in summer. As water temperatures in the Bay and its tributaries drop in the fall, the cooling surface waters, which are well-oxygenated from contact with the air, increase in density and sink to the bottom, bringing up deep water and allowing it to be reoxygenated. Stormy weather, with winds and rain, adds more oxygen.

Summertime oxygen concentrations are low in the deep waters of the Bay and some of its tributaries, but in winter they are much higher. Thus these deep waters are stable, relatively warm, and well-oxygenated, so they represent the best cold-weather fish habitat in the system for most species. Many of the fish that winter in the Chesapeake can be found in these areas, especially forage species like anchovies and silversides, and larger species like rockfish and white perch.

Some fish leave the Bay altogether. Anyone seeking bluefish, trout, spot, croaker, or summer flounder will be disappointed. With the onset of cold weather, these species head for an even more stable environment than the Bay: the Atlantic Ocean. They winter offshore out on the continental shelf, returning to the Cheasapeake's rich feeding grounds when the weather warms up. Most menhaden, which are major forage for blues and trout, also head for the ocean, though a few schools will stay in deep holes in the Bay.

Some cold-blooded animals are dormant in winter. In late fall, crabs seek out holes and channels, where they bury in the bottom mud. Snapping turtles and diamondback terrapins hibernate in the mud too. Shellfish like oysters and clams continue to feed, but their food intake slows down with their metabolisms. There is less feed available to them anyway, since plankton populations are low now (which also results in winter's characteristically clear water).

If early spring is an acquired taste, the dead of winter is even more so. For most of the Chesapeake's creatures, it is a time of sleep or inactivity. The only master winter fishermen, the Bay's watermen, were active in years past, but declining oyster and rockfish stocks have slowed them down badly.

For the rest of us, winter is a time for quiet pursuits and reflection. Boating should be confined to small waterways and calm days. Explorers should wear warm clothes and good life jackets, carry extra clothes in waterproof bags, and pack unbreakable Thermos bottles full of hot, cheering, nonalcoholic beverages. Itineraries should be unambitious. Travel should be punctuated by stops to get out of the wind and have hot drinks. Tea and cookies is a staple for this season. Sitting in the sun makes for a good time to watch and contemplate.

A friend who teaches art history in Richmond remarked once that the way to understand a painting is to "stare at it 'til you get bored, and then look at it for ten more minutes." That is good advice for poking around the Bay in winter. It is the best time to learn to look. Stripped to their bare bones, creeks and marshes show up small details that are easy to overlook in richer seasons.

Otter trails and muskrat leads are good examples. They show up well when vegetation is at a minimum. The spots where otters climb out of the water, for example, are not always big, obvious slides. Sometimes they are merely depressions on the bank at the edges of thickets. Honeysuckle and cordgrass keep such places hidden at other times.

Another enlightening activity is picking through stubble on the marsh. Most of the plants are surprisingly recognizable, and some of their seeds will show up on the surface of the mud, especially in tidal fresh marshes. It is much easier in winter to understand how marsh plants weather, break up, and wash out into the creeks than it is in summer when everything is green and lush. The brittle stubble appears dry and lifeless, but it is a major part of the soup that will feed the hordes of bacteria, copepods, and other plankton upon which the water's food webs will depend in spring.

Another good contemplative exercise is scanning the sky for birds. As always, bald eagles and other soaring birds do not advertise their presence, nor do many ducks until they get close. Canada geese and tundra swans, of course, are exceptions.

Winter is a good time to watch water currents. Somehow it is easier to see them now than in warm weather. Only the most experienced physical oceanographers understand the Bay system's water currents in detail, and they would be the first to say that their knowledge is far from comprehensive. But it is quite possible for the patient and careful lay observer to puzzle out the workings of a particular curve or eddy. Such small-scale understanding is always directly useful to fishermen, but the insight is satisfying to anyone.

The trick to winter poking is, then, to go out dressed comfortably under carefully chosen circumstances and open yourself quietly but patiently to the waterway you are exploring. The same basic instructions apply in summer, but somehow it is easier to learn to follow them in winter. Let this lean season be your teacher.

Tidal Fresh Rivers—Confine your wintertime small boat explorations to protected waters and keep your trips short. Tidal fresh creeks are good choices. Stay off the big rivers. They are deceptively powerful, especially if swollen by winter rains.

In creeks, look especially for waterfowl, bald eagles, marsh hawks, and other birds. Otters, muskrats, and raccoons are all active, though it always takes a sharp eye to read their signs. Stubble on the marsh is worth poking through, but be careful walking. A wet leg is no big deal in June, and it can be a comfort in August, but it is an invitation to hypothermia in February.

Fish are mostly dormant, schooled in deep holes. Surprisingly, though, several species of panfish can be caught, and their flavor seems to be enhanced by the cold water. Look for white and yellow perch in the deepest water in the creek. If the hole adjoins a mudflat with southern exposure and the day is warm, you may also find a few whites in the shallow water foraging minnows and grass shrimp. Use a tiny jig tipped with bait for this fishing. In the holes, fish bait on the bottom. By the way, check the laws on yellow perch. Their numbers are down, and catch restrictions may apply.

One fish that is surprisingly active in winter is the chain pickerel, nicknamed "pike." It seems to thrive on cold water. Waterways like the Chickahominy River in Virginia and Tuckahoe Creek in Maryland have strong pickerel populations. Minnows are the prime bait for them in winter. Fish one under a bobber on the Chickahominy and as a sweetener to a jig on the Tuckahoe. Check with a good local tackle shop for details.

Brackish Rivers and Salt Marshes—Except for warm-blooded animals, activity is minimal in these areas. Keep all boating confined to small creeks and marsh guts. Do not venture out onto open waters.

If this section seems to dwell on caution, it is because we have profound respect for the dangers of cold water. They cannot be overemphasized.

But there are ways to take winter on its own terms and still get outside. Described above are several that minimize risk, and here is another.

Walks—There is one more activity worth your consideration—walking. A large number of public areas in the Bay country offer excellent walking trails that allow good winter explorations along a broad variety of waterways.

For these explorations, a good pair of waterproof boots can be as useful as a boat. Add warm clothes, but work with layers so you can take off something if the day is sunny and the walking warms you up. Carry a day pack with a Thermos, lunch, binoculars, field guides, and extra clothing.

Below is a list of our favorite winter walking areas, with telephone numbers to call for further information.

Virginia

Seashore State Park, Virginia Beach: Good beach and marsh trails. 757-481-2131

York River State Park, Croaker: Good trail along Taskinas Creek. 757-566-3036

Presquile National Wildlife Refuge: Good trail on island, especially edge of swamp and marsh. Access only by ferry. 804-733-8042

James River Park, Richmond: Extensive trails at the fall line. 804-780-5733

Ragged Island Creek Wildlife Management Area, Isle of Wight County (across the James from Newport News): Large salt marsh with extensive trails. 804-367-1000

Westmoreland State Park, Montross: Good beach with fossils near the Stratford Bluffs on the Potomac. 804-493-8821

Mason Neck State Park, Lorton: Extensive trail system on the upper Potomac. Park may be closed due to nesting eagles. 703-550-0960

George Washington Parkway and Dyke Marsh, Alexandria: Long trail system on the Potomac from Alexandria to Mount Vernon. Open all year with designated parking areas.

Maryland

Patuxent River Park, Upper Marlboro: Extensive trail system along the tidal fresh section of the Patuxent River and Mattaponi Creek. 301-627-6075

Sandy Point State Park, Annapolis: Good winter beachcombing. 410-974-2149

Elk Neck State Park, Elkton: Extensive trails along shore at the head of the Bay. 410-287-5333

Eastern Neck Island National Wildlife Refuge, Rock Hall: Good trail system on island at the mouth of Chester River. Accessible by bridge. 410-639-7056

Blackwater National Wildlife Refuge, Cambridge: Good trails, excellent wildlife drive and visitor center. Lots of waterfowl and eagles. 410-228-2677

Pocomoke River State Park, Shad Landing Area, Snow Hill: Good trail along Pocomoke River and neighboring swamp. 410-632-2566

Pocomoke River State Park, Milburn Landing Area, Pocomoke City: Across and downriver from Shad Landing. Good trail. 410-632-2566

The Chesapeake Bay: Problems and Possibilities

By now, it must be clear that the Bay system is large and diverse. If you have spent any time around it, you know that it is no longer a pristine wilderness, that in some areas its water quality has declined, and that its stocks of living resources are reduced. How did this state of affairs come to be? Who is to blame? How do we fix it?

A noted Bay scientist recently remarked, "If you change the character of your land, you change the character of your runoff." There are 13 million of us in the Chesapeake watershed, with 3 million more projected to arrive in the next thirty years. We use the land around the Bay intensively for a broad variety of activities. We use the water after it has fallen as rain in the watershed but before it runs into the Bay, and we use it once it is there, for cooling, for cleaning, and for waste disposal. We affect water in ways that we don't even think about—stormwater runoff from streets, runoff from farm fields and suburban lawns, and runoff from construction sites all pick up toxics, plant nutrients (nitrogen and phosphorus), and soil. Impervious surfaces like rooftops and parking lots accelerate the process. Point source discharges from sewage treatment plants and industrial plants add more nitrogen and phosphorus, plus compounds that range from motor oils to heavy metals. Almost every human activity affects the condition of the Chesapeake Bay system. Unless we deal with these materials before they get into the waterways, we pay a price in the condition of the Bay.

The problems that our activities produce are as varied as the activities themselves. Soil runoff literally fills up waterways. This is especially true in the upper tidal reaches, where downstream currents slow and rivers widen in response to the inflow of water on the tides. The Bay system is a trap, a settling basin. This feature is a two-edged sword that accounts for its biological richness but also for its vulnerability to the accumulated pressures of all of us. Collection of soil is obvious, but both toxics and nutrients accumulate as well.

In limnology, the study of lakes, there is a well-known phenomenon called eutrophication, an aging process in which waterways gradually accumulate nutrients and soils and change from clear, deep basins to turbid, shallow ones. Fishery managers and some sportfishermen have known for years that reservoirs age. No one ever believed that the Bay could age. It was believed simply to be too large a system. Over the past fifteen years, however, it has become painfully obvious that we are indeed capable of aging the Bay and have done so.

The water is too rich. That sounds like a paradox, but what happens, in simple terms, is that as high levels of nitrogen and phosphorus become available and as the water becomes cloudy with soil, the plant community shifts its balance away from a diverse group of rooted aquatic plants (submerged aquatic vegetation) and some algae to a preponderance of brown, green, and blue-green algae. The total biomass (living material) may actually be greater, but the community species structure, including both plants and animals, has shifted. From our point of view, the mix has changed away from the creatures that are most valuable to us, like submerged grasses, rockfish, and shad, to creatures that are less desirable, like planktonic algae that cloud the water and cause problems for other creatures.

Eutrophication is a subject where the details are very subtle but the outlines are clear. It is difficult for us laypeople to study individual phytoplankton species, but they may well have profound effects on the diets of filter-feeding animals like oysters. It is well documented that they reduce ambient light in the waterways and thus kill off submerged vegetation. It is difficult to establish direct cause and effect relationships in all cases, although some can be shown.

This much is clear: We affect the Bay system in many ways.

Virtually all of us play roles in the problem. There is a great tendency to point fingers, for example, at farmers or at industry, but we demand unblemished food at low prices and consumer products that contain toxics of which we are not even aware.

There are solutions to all of the problems, and creative approaches to using them can provide more cost-effective solutions. Conventional nitrogen removal from sewage, for example, is so expensive to install, operate, and maintain that it is not feasible in most sewage treatment plants around the Bay. There are, however, a number of bacteria-based biological removal processes that show great promise.

Finding solutions will take broad, long-term commitment from the public to support the government cleanup programs. That process is well begun, and it must continue. There are several sources of further information about the Bay cleanup and what you can do to get involved, especially *Turning the Tide: Saving the Chesapeake Bay* by Tom Horton and Bill Eichbaum. See "Books" in Chapter 4 for details.

Our Bay is hurt, but it is not dead. There is still a lot of love. We're the problem, but we're also the solution. It is exciting to be part of the cleanup, to give something back to this amazing waterway that so enriches our lives. Contact the Chesapeake Bay Foundation (410-268-8816) for ways to get involved.

three

Good Boats

The Chesapeake Bay Foundation's original canoe fleet has logged over 1,800 field trips in the last seventeen years. The boats have covered over 7,000 miles on the water and have carried something over 35,000 students. The trailer has traveled well over 200,000 miles on the road. These canoes have been on every major river system of the Bay. It is difficult to overestimate how valuable they have been. They have probably logged more miles poking around in tributaries of the Bay system than any other small boats in the region. For us, they are the archetypal vessels for the small boat explorer.

They are not alone in their utility, however. Other kinds of boats also serve well for purposes of exploring. This chapter will discuss the whole range.

It is a good general principle that the best boat on any given day is a safe one that will allow you to do what you want to do. Safety and utility are the watchwords. Safety will be discussed in the section of this chapter entitled "Experience and How to Get It Safely." A boat that is too big will get in the way of what you are trying to do, but don't pick one that is too small to be safe. Remember that your boat is your vehicle. It's not the primary experience. You are out there on the water to explore, and look, and listen. Having a good boat as a partner is a great feeling, but remember that the boat is there to serve you. Be pragmatic.

Chesapeake Bay Foundation canoes on Rosier Creek, Virginia. For nearly twenty years, students have used CBF's Grumman 17s to explore every river system on the Chesapeake. Photo by the author.

Self-Propelled Craft

Canoes

A canoe for poking around should be big enough to carry a large load, stable for standing up and looking around (when appropriate) and for climbing into and out of, and seaworthy. It should have a keel or a V-bottom, and the bottom should have a straight run for good tracking in wind. Speed is not terribly important, as you won't be covering great distances, but a boat that performs poorly is a trial to the spirit, especially when you have to paddle into the wind or tide, or both.

It should be understandable that I favor seventeen-foot standard-keel Grumman aluminum canoes, for CBF's canoe fleets include several dozen of them. The virtues of a well-designed aluminum canoe are durability, stability, seaworthiness, and reasonable speed. It may not be pretty, and it can be noisy if you are careless with feet, paddles, and the like. It is, however, a very good basic vehicle for exploring small waters.

When ABS plastic canoes came out, they were hailed as the boats of the future. They are quiet, and the flexible hull material keeps them from hanging up and denting on rocks or fallen logs. Unfortunately, it is difficult to build an ABS boat with a keel. The lack of a keel is not a great problem if the hull is well designed and is carrying some weight, as the hull form will help the boat to track properly in the wind. A more serious problem is the fact that the bottom, lacking the stiffness of a keel, will "oil can," or move up and down with ripples in the water. This movement creates drag, which makes many ABS boats noticeably slower in flat water than hulls with rigid bottoms.

Most ABS canoes are designed to be paddled on flowing rivers, especially in white water. In my experience, they do not adapt well to tidal rivers. The exceptions are boats made with V-sections molded into the bottom. The V aids in tracking and also gives the bottom a measure of rigiditity. The V-bottomed ABS canoes that I have paddled are wonderful. They are expensive, and I would not like to put them through the rigors of institutional use; but for personal boats, they are excellent.

I have generally not been impressed with the fiberglass boats that I have seen, although I may not have seen enough of them to give them a fair test. If well designed and well built, they have handled satisfactorily, but they don't seem to have any major advantages over the aluminum boats, and they lack aluminum's durability.

To sum up, a properly equipped canoe is probably the best all-around exploring boat. It is portable, capable of covering a broad variety of waterways, and able to carry lots of gear. Quiet, slow, self-propelled travel brings one into close touch with small rivers and creeks. It is fair to say that each of us involved in this book has learned the basics of exploring tidal rivers and creeks in canoes.

Kayaks

Speed can be useful, and sea kayaks are quick. They can't carry a lot of bulky gear, and they are not stable enough for standing up and throwing a cast net, but they are very seaworthy. It takes more training to use a sea kayak effectively and safely than it does to paddle a canoe. For that reason, they are not good entry-level exploring boats. If, however, you are already quite comfortable on all-day trips in canoes under a variety of conditions, you may find it worth your while to try one out. If you grant their limitations, they are excellent watercraft for poking around tidal rivers and creeks. Only a few sporting goods stores carry them, but those that do usually have a deep commitment to teaching customers how to use the boats. There is also an active association of sea kayakers on the Bay, the Chesapeake Association of Sea Kayakers (CASK). Several of its active members are addicted to paddling marsh creeks. If these boats sound intriguing, by all means contact the association through a local kayak dealer.

Rowboats

Like sea kayaks, good rowboats offer speed along with closeness to the water. Whether your boat has a fixed or sliding seat, the feeling of pulling a well-designed oar and having the boat surge under you is a thrill. Appropriate models depend on your skill level and the water you pick, but they range from recreational shells to fixed-seat skiffs. There are plenty of models to choose from.

There are three disadvantages to rowing. First, the rower must face backward. It is reasonable to watch the river from behind most of the time, but there are times when it is useful to face forward. Another problem is having two oars sticking out, hampering movement in narrow places. Finally, most good rowboats are too narrow to stand up in comfortably to pole.

Nonetheless, the disadvantages don't necessarily outweigh the feeling of watching a river unwind behind you as your boat glides along. If you have a good rowboat, pick your water carefully and go exploring.

Techniques for Self-Propelled Craft

Canoeing on Tidal Rivers

Strong winds and tides are facts of life on tidal rivers, to be taken advantage of when possible and endured when not. Great strength is useful but not necessary. What *is* necessary is developing efficient paddling skills that make the most of the strength you do have. Over the years, we at CBF have cheerfully borrowed ideas and techniques, adapted them, and made up new ones as we have gone along. A canoe is one of the world's most useful boats to begin with, but we find that the techniques described here will make that good boat better. Developing tidal water paddling skills is a satisfying experience.

The Bow Stroke—Despite its name, this is for both bow and stern paddlers. It is simply the power part of any forward stroke. For most tidewater paddling, we favor long, easy strokes that use the paddle to take advantage of leverage from the arms, shoulders, and back. Six points will help you develop such a stroke:

1. Make sure your paddle is long enough for good leverage. In general, a good tidewater paddle should be a little longer than a good white water paddle. It should also have a little flex. The Maine guide model, made of solid ash with its distinctive wide, tapered handle, is out of fashion and hard to find today, but it is a great flat water tool. The guides on the big glacial lakes up there know exactly what they need. Some aluminum and plastic paddles also have some flex, and they are reasonable substitutes.

    If you are in the stern, a paddle of correct length should stretch your arms out fully from side to side, with your fingertips just wrapped around the handle and the blade tip. In the bow, it can be three inches or so shorter.

2. Put the handle in the palm of your upper hand and grip the shaft at the throat (where the blade and shaft meet) with your lower hand. This grip should put your hands about six inches farther apart than your shoulders are wide and give you the leverage you need.

3. Make sure you keep your lower arm straight during the stroke. Doing so will force you to pull with your *latissimus dorsi* muscles, the ones that run across your back below the shoulder blades.

4. Your upper hand should start by your ear and push forward at chin level until straight, like punching an imaginary bag in front of you.

Continue by bringing it down smoothly to belt level. This movement ensures a long, smooth stroke with lots of leverage from the hand pushing the handle of the paddle.

5. Make sure the paddle shaft is as nearly vertical as possible, to keep your lower hand from banging the side of the boat.

6. At the end of the stroke, the paddle blade will be lying on the water like a beaver's tail. Lift it a couple of inches and swing it away from the boat to recover, keeping it flat all the way. This move is called feathering, and it saves a lot of work lifting the blade unnecessarily high and pushing it against the wind. That's a small point, but over a full day, it can save plenty of energy.

Stroke descriptions are tedious to read. It may help as you read along to get a paddle and go through the motions (gently if you are indoors). Then work to get comfortable with the paddle on the water.

Steering—This is a critical skill. Once the boat is moving, you, the stern person, have to be able to make it go where you want it to go. The most efficient way to do that is with a system called the J-stroke, but it takes practice. There is an easier way to start, with the rudder stroke.

At the end of a standard bow stroke, when the paddle blade is lying flat on the water, simply turn it to vertical, so it is like a ship's rudder in the water. You may find it easiest to think of turning your upper hand so that your thumb points to the sky. Use the rudder to steer the boat by pressing out, away from the boat, or by reaching out and pulling it in toward the boat. In effect, you are making little sideways strokes at right angles to your direction of travel. As always, the easiest way to pick up the technique is to use it.

Two pointers will make the rudder movements easier. Remember to keep your steering strokes at right angles to the boat, and remember to trail the paddle. It is your steering wheel. Every forward stroke you take will drive the boat off course, so you must correct your course constantly. It takes concentration to pick up the technique, but, once acquired, it becomes a habit, something you do as needed without thinking much about it, at the end of every stroke. Remember that the shortest distance between two points is a straight line.

Dealing with a head wind requires constant attention. It is crucial to keep the boat moving. It is also crucial to be especially careful about steering.

A tandem paddling crew can do quite well on a tidal river if the bow person has a strong bow stroke and the stern person puts a good rudder on the end of each stroke. Many people paddle this way happily all their lives. If it works for you and you are satisfied, that is fine.

You may find in time, though, that trailing the blade on the rudder means that you take fewer strokes than your partner in the bow does. Moreover, you will discover that if bow and stern paddlers can synchronize their strokes, the boat will move faster with less effort. To synchronize with your bow paddler, you must develop a J-stroke.

The J-stroke is a quick outward rotation of the paddle blade at the end of a normal stroke. In contrast to the rudder, concentrate on turning your upper hand out and down so that your thumb points toward the water. At the same time, with your lower hand press the blade away from the boat. Normally the quick outward thrust of the blade will counteract the natural tendency of the canoe to turn away from the side that the stern person is paddling on.

It definitely takes time on the water to develop a comfortable J-stroke, but part of the feel comes from getting comfortable with the rudder. Anyone who has a good rudder stroke can pick up the J in a day of poking around on still water. As always, concentration is important. At first, the outward thrust of the paddle may make your bottom arm shoulder joint sore, but the pain is part of a natural loosening-up process, and it will go away.

After a day or so of using the J-stroke, you will develop a feel for how much hook you need to put on the end of the stroke to compensate for normal steerage and any additional effects from wind and tide. Under some conditions, you will find that you actually need to reach out and pull in with the blade.

As your sense of the boat develops, you will find that you never make a pure stroke. There will always be some little push or pull sideways at the end. You'll be doing whatever it takes to keep your boat on course, and you'll be making small corrections on every stroke. You may have to shorten your stroke slightly, but these quick little hooks will allow you to synchronize with your bow paddler. The combination of constantly being on course and being synchronized will allow you to cover water with a minimum of effort, allowing you plenty of opportunity to watch what is going on around you.

When the stern person is stronger than or equal to the bow person, the boat will turn away from the side the stern person is paddling on. A stronger bow paddler will pull the boat around the other way, toward the stern person. Then the J-stroke will cause the boat to veer even farther off course. This is normally what happens to couples when the woman takes the stern and the man the bow. There is a common misconception that men should always paddle in the stern and women in the bow. Often the boat is more efficient the other way around. It simply takes a different steering stroke, called a modified pull. Here is how it works.

At the beginning of your stroke, reach the blade forward and out, away from the boat. Put the blade into the water and pull diagonally in toward the boat for the first half of the stroke. When the blade gets close to the boat, turn it to pull straight back as you would on a normal bow stroke. Do not make a J at the end. This is a powerful, efficient stroke that you may find easier to learn than the J. Having both the modified pull and the J will allow you to work efficiently with any bow paddler, large or small. You may also find the modified pull useful in some crosswinds (see below).

Pivots—In rapids, it is dangerous to turn a canoe even slightly sideways to the current, so white water paddlers have developed a system of techniques to slide a boat sideways to maneuver around rocks and other obstructions. The strokes are the draw, the cross draw, and the pry or pushaway, all designed to move one end of the boat sideways.

If the strokes used by bow and stern persons both move the boat in the same direction, it will slide sideways. If the combination is reversed, however, the strokes move the bow and stern in opposite directions, so the boat will pivot in a tight circle, just the right move for sharp curves in winding tidal creeks.

For the draw stroke, simply reach out sideways with the paddle. Pull it sideways toward the boat, bringing the blade in with the lower hand and pushing the handle out with the upper hand. As the blade reaches the side of the boat, slice it up to the rear to bring it out of the water. This last step is important, for the boat will be moving sideways and will catch the blade underneath if you don't pick it up.

Practice the draw in a protected place. It does involve leaning out of the boat with the paddle. The stroke may feel awkward at first, but using it will make you comfortable soon enough.

To move the bow the other way without switching hands on the paddle, use the cross draw. Simply swing the paddle to the other side and execute a draw there, but raise the blade out of the water toward the bow instead of to the rear as you did in the draw. The cross draw sounds and looks thoroughly awkward until you have done it six times. By then, you will appreciate it. It's a handy technique and a strong stroke.

The pushaway is simply a draw in reverse, beginning with swinging the blade into the water from the rear. It is best used in the stern. Instead of pulling the paddle toward the boat, you push it away. The pushaway too becomes comfortable with practice.

In combination, a draw each at the bow and the stern will make the boat pivot one way. A cross draw and a pushaway pivot it the other way. A good tandem crew can develop quite a satisfying sense of teamwork negotiating a creek or a marsh gut.

Dealing with Wind and Current—Wind and tide are inevitable. If you spend much time on the Bay and its tributaries, you will get it all: calms, choppy water, head winds, tail winds, head tides, fair tides. When paddling is easy, appreciate it. When it isn't, compensate as best you can and endure it. Most times, what you see when you are on the water will be more than worth the work. There are several techniques that will make things easier:

Steering—With a head wind (a common occurrence in a narrow channel), be very careful to keep your boat on course, or it will be blown off sideways. A quartering wind (coming toward you at an angle) will work constantly to blow it sideways. This condition is most easily dealt with by having the stern person paddle on the leeward (downwind) side and the bow person on the upwind side. The stern person will actually have to steer less because the wind will counteract the boat's tendency to turn. If the wind is very strong, the bow person is in a position to make a draw stroke from time to time to help keep the boat on course.

Sometimes a wind that quarters at an acute angle will blow the stern off course more than the bow. Under that condition, you will feel that you are working overly hard to steer on the downwind side. Switch sides and use the modified pull steering stroke instead of the rudder or the J.

After some time on the water, you will gain a sense of how hard you need to work to steer in calm waters. Use this sense to help you decide which side to paddle on in a head wind. If you've picked the correct side, you'll know that you are working less to steer, even if you are still working hard to paddle forward.

Trimming the Boat—In general, distribute weight in the canoe as evenly as possible so that it floats level. In a headwind, balance it so that it is slightly lower in the bow than in the stern. The wind will work more on the stern than on the bow, tending to blow it downwind and thus keep the boat on course. In a strong tailwind, reverse the configuration. Be sure, though, not to get the bow or stern too low to deal with whatever waves there are.

Picking your Course—Watch the patterns of wind, waves, and current flow on the water surface. If you are going against wind or current, take advantage of lees (calmer, protected areas) and eddies (current swirls and reversals) whenever possible. In general, the current will be stronger on the outsides of curves and weaker on the insides.

Ferrying—In general, it is best to take large waves and strong winds by paddling directly into them or quartering slightly off them. Just as in white water, it is risky to turn the boat sideways to them. Even when you're traveling directly across the current, keep the bow well into the wind. If you do, you will find that the boat moves gently sideways, crab fashion. The bow person's job is simply to paddle forward at a moderate pace, just to keep the boat moving. The stern person paddles forward too, but pays strict attention to maintaining the boat's angle with respect to the wind. The technique is borrowed directly from white water paddling. It is a good practical exercise in vector physics.

Sitting versus Kneeling—In very rough water, always kneel on the bottom of the boat, with your buttocks resting on a seat or thwart. This lowers the boat's center of gravity, making it as stable as possible. Normally, though, on tidal waters it is safe enough and more comfortable to sit on the seats. It is best to sit on the forward edge of the seat, with your knees dropped in front of you and your ankles crossed. The position keeps your weight fairly low and your back straight.

Double-Bladed Paddles —The remarks above apply to solo paddling as well as to tandem paddling, but going solo with a conventional single blade can be quite difficult on tidal waters. We recommend strongly that you use a nine- to ten-foot double-bladed paddle when going solo. It will give you excellent boat control even in high winds, and good speed to boot. Paddling with a double blade is more work than with a single, but it can still be reduced to an easy, efficient pace, and it feels good. It is a delightful way to travel.

Set the paddle blades at a right angle to each other. Grip the shaft with your hands about twelve inches farther apart than the width of your shoulders. Set one hand at a right angle to its blade and hold the shaft loosely enough to pivot in the other. Take a stroke with the fixed hand and as you raise the blade from the water, flex that wrist upward smartly. This will bring the other blade into position for you to take a stroke with it. Do so and, at the end, put your wrist back into position for the first blade. The process, like the draw and the cross draw, sounds awkward at first, but a few minutes' practice on land will get you comfortable with it.

The basic motion with the double blade is the same as with the single blade: pull back with your lower arm as you push forward with your upper arm. Stroking successively on opposite sides will keep the boat basically on course, but sweeping a blade in a small arc at the end of a stroke will make course corrections. Use larger arcs to make turns. The double blade can be used to make pushaways, draws, and even cross draws for pivots and slides. It is an unconventional canoe tool, but an extremely effective one.

The double blade is basically a tool for solo paddling, but two of them can be used in tandem. If the paddlers work well together, the boat will be very fast. We have a continuing debate about whether to coordinate paddles on the opposite or same side on each stroke. If you are trying it, you have enough skill to pick your own preference.

Push-Poles

In the state of Maine, poles are considered nearly as important as paddles, especially when going upstream. Our tidal rivers aren't as wild as the Allagash, but it can be difficult to paddle against the current in twelve inches of water over a sand bottom in the upper ends of the creeks. In that kind of situation, a pole can make a canoe fly.

Poling is another technique best practiced in protected water. Stand behind and brace your shins against the stern thwart, if you have a passenger, or stand in front of it and brace with your calves if you are solo. Hold the pole with your hands palm up, put the base of the pole on the creek bottom, and push back, gently at first. At the end of the stroke, trail the pole like a rudder to hold the canoe on course. Then smoothly raise the pole and repeat the process.

In Maine, a pole is simply a sapling cut in the woods and fitted with a metal shoe to keep it from splitting. A handy alternative here on the Chesapeake is to pick up a broken-off oyster tong shaft and cut it down to eight feet. Such shafts can often be had for the asking in watermen's communities and around seafood packing houses. Such a pole will be flat on one side and rounded on the other, about three inches wide at the bottom. It works well on a hard bottom and can even be used as a stand-up paddle.

If you can't find a tong shaft, buy a fir closet pole from a building supply store. If you have a problem with it splitting at the end, soak it in fiberglass resin and let it cure. If you find that it sinks into the bottom too deeply, bolt a $3 \times 5 \times 6$-inch triangle cut from a 2×4 onto the butt of the pole, with the 5-inch side against the pole and the 3-inch side even with the end.

Whether you use a tong shaft or a closet pole, treat it with linseed or tung oil to make it feel better in your hands.

Sooner or later, you will figure out everything in this chapter on your own. Although these suggestions are shortcuts, each has a specific purpose. Get comfortable with them and you will find them useful. The whole purpose is to get the boat to do what you want it to do. Go spend some time on the water.

Powerboats

Some Thoughts about Speed and Powerboats

Bill Portlock, Janet Harvey, and I would be the first to tell you how important it is to explore slowly. Quiet, self-propelled travel is the best way to acquaint yourself with the Bay's intimate waterways. Nothing will bring you into closer touch with them than a canoe, kayak, or rowboat.

With that said, though, we must add that speed has its place. Time is what dictates that fact. Access to Bay waterways is generally good. Sometimes, though, you may want to explore more of a particular waterway than you have time to paddle or row it. Once you get to know several waterways that are close together, you may want to see how they fit together. Twelve to twenty knots of speed can be very useful in such situations.

The most important thing to be aware of when traveling at higher speeds is to adjust your perspective. Self-propelled travel will force you to look closely around you. Traveling with a motor behind can insulate you if you are not careful. You will see below that we have some very strong prejudices about what kinds of powerboats are appropriate for exploring creeks and rivers.

Tin Boats

Back when CBF first started running canoe trips, there was a big need to scout new trip areas, and there was very seldom time to do so by spending a day exploring each waterway in a canoe. I had an old ten-horsepower outboard, so I started scouring the newspapers for a secondhand aluminum skiff to go with it. The idea was to buy the biggest boat that I could get on and off the roof of the truck easily. Most aluminum boat companies make at least one lightweight cartop model that is fourteen feet long but weighs less than 150 pounds. The one that I found weighs about 130. It is certainly more than I would like to raise up over my head all at one time, but I worked out a simple system in which I never had to lift more than half of it at once. It is easy enough to slide along the ground until it is alongside the truck. I lift the bow end up onto the rack while the stern stays on the ground. Then I lift the stern, slide the whole boat up onto the rack, and tie it down. Removing it is the reverse. I bought a good set of oars for the boat and found a broken oyster tong shaft, which I shortened to eight feet to serve as a push-pole.

That skiff has been to almost as many places as CBF's original canoe fleet. With the combination of motor, oars, and pole, it can go anywhere that a canoe will go, and it has the added advantage of cruising at twelve to fifteen knots. It does not row particularly well, but the oars are there primarily for emergencies anyway. The old ten-horse has gone to its reward, but it has been replaced by a modern eight-horse which is just as powerful, burns half the fuel, and has an excellent shallow-drive bracket that allows the whole rig to run in no more than ten inches of water. The motor is reasonably quiet, but when I want to be absolutely silent, the push-pole does an excellent job. One other piece of gear that is very important is an extension tiller that allows me to sit on the middle seat and thus balance the boat while operating it.

This kind of skiff is not worth much out in the open Bay, but in almost any of the tributaries it is a tough, versatile, and economical workhorse. When I was running canoe trips, I carried it on one side of the rack of the truck, with an extra canoe leaning up against it at an angle. If I had a trip scheduled in unfamiliar water, I could run the previous day's trip, then load the canoes, drive to the new location, and put the tin boat overboard. Within two hours at the new field trip site, I could scout the water and work out the next day's format effectively.

The tin boat gave me some beautiful evenings on the rivers and saved a lot of lost days of work. I remember one day when it was especially useful. I scouted the whole length of the Pocomoke River, from Snow Hill down t o Pocomoke Sound. That trip did take the whole day, because I scouted four different potential field trips. In another case, I scouted three different sites on the Chester River in one day, pulling the boat out of the water after exploring one and then relaunching it at the next.

Not all tin boats need to be built as lightly as mine is. Aluminum skiffs come in sizes from ten to eighteen feet, in a variety of dimensions and with varying degrees of hull thickness. They also come as johnboats with flat or slight V-bottoms and bows. I tend to favor semi-V-hulls rather than johnboats, simply because they are better sea boats, but for the calmer waters of the upper rivers, good johnboats are hard to beat. They are stable, and they can carry a lot of weight.

In either V-hulls or johnboats, I steer away from ten- and twelve-foot models. It is personal prejudice, but I don't think these boats are big enough for one adult, let alone two. A fourteen-foot boat can handle two to three people, depending on their size and the boat's beam. A sixteen-foot boat is a good all-around choice for creeks and rivers and for some open water as well. A well-designed sixteen-footer will carry four adults easily. Eighteen-foot tin boats are hard to find, but they are very useful, especially on the lower rivers. With care, they can be run in the open Bay as well.

Engine size is something of a personal preference. With a light-weight fourteen-foot boat, an eight-horse is an excellent choice. Wider, deeper fourteen-footers and lighter sixteen-footers do well with ten- and fifteen-horsepower engines. A wide, deep sixteen-footer will do well with a twenty or twenty-five. Forty horsepower seems to be a good all-around size for an eighteen-foot V-hull or johnboat, although with care paid to loading and weight distribution, a twenty-five-horse can suffice there as well. Avoid underpowering the boat, but do not take as gospel a salesman's dictum that the boat needs to be able to cruise at twenty-five knots easily. Most of the time, all you will want to be able to do is lift its intended load so that the hull planes (skims over the water) at three-quarters throttle.

If you opt for a tin boat, be sure, as noted above, that it has oars, a push-pole, and an extension tiller. You might also consider a pair of removable swivel chairs for the midships seat.

If you buy one of the larger boats, you will have to carry it on a trailer. This is no great disadvantage. Any trailer carrying a tin boat is a relatively simple one that can be towed by a small and economical automobile.

A good center console skiff. This one happens to be School, *the author's veteran Mako 17. Photo by Bill Portlock.*

Aluminum skiffs are simple, unpretentious boats. They are tough, easy to care for, economical, and very useful. For many kinds of exploring, they are top choices.

Center Console Skiffs

A friend of mine in the marine publishing business coined a phrase for boats that can be run safely in open water but are still small enough to use in confined waterways. He calls them "seven-league boots." Seventeen- to twenty-foot open outboard skiffs with center steering consoles fit this category to a T.

It is no accident that Bill Portlock and I own boats of this type. I have, in fact, owned mine for twenty years and did some major work on it four years ago. I thought hard about selling the boat before undertaking the big project, but the truth is that even after all that time, there was nothing on the market that I would cheerfully swap it for. After four seasons of running it in its reincarnated condition, I still feel the same way. A boat of this type is simply too useful to let go.

Both our skiffs are top-quality models from major manufacturers. Both are fiberglass and, coincidentally, both have ninety-horsepower outboards, though I have run mine with as little as sixty. Both are excellent sea boats, but neither draws more than eight inches with the engine tilted up. It should be no surprise that each is equipped with a good push-pole.

These boats, and others like them, are just big enough to run standing up, and they are designed to be comfortable that way, with plenty of walking-around space and sturdy grab rails for handholds. When running in big seas, it is much more comfortable to stand, so that one's legs can flex with the movement of the hull. This behavior is *not* recommended in boats not designed for it, but it is a major selling point on these hulls. Another important selling point from a safety standpoint is that both of our boats are self-bailing. Their drain plugs can be removed in heavy seas so that any water which comes aboard will drain out.

These boats can take more rough water than the people in them can comfortably stand. After a full day of fishing out in the open Bay, we feel as though we have been on horseback for eight hours, but we are safe. The boats are not fast in rough water. Neither does well above twenty knots in a chop, and in high waves, we must pull them back to fifteen knots or below. I have recently fitted mine with hydraulic trim tabs, which help a lot in big seas.

The reason for the engine size we have chosen is to find a compromise between having enough power to keep from overstraining the engine with a full load aboard and the desire to save fuel. An undersized engine can actually burn more fuel because it is working hard all the time. At the same time, there is no point in powering the boat so that its top speed is over forty knots—we rarely operate much faster than twenty. An added benefit is that any engine under 100 horsepower will idle down to very low speeds, which is important in easing the boats up small creeks.

In addition to their abilities in open water, these skiffs are excellent platforms for exploring creeks and rivers. One major advantage is that during the day, those aboard can stand up, stretch their legs, and walk around. A boat of this type will have a comfortable seat built into the front of the console or will mount a well-padded cooler there as a seat. Some also have comfortable helm chairs, although I have been very happy without a helm chair on mine for as long as I have owned it.

It is important to be thoughtful about speed in these boats. When they are lifted up on plane, skimming over the surface, they tow very little wake, and going slowly at idle, they tow very little wake. At intermediate speeds, however, when they are climbing up onto plane, they tow very large seas and are most inefficient. These intermediate speeds should be avoided. If you are in a tight place where twenty knots is too fast, then slow the boat 'way down. You will be operating at kayak speed at least, if not at canoe speed, enabling you to do some productive looking. If you are running at low speed, your engine will be sipping fuel, so your travel will be relatively economical.

As may be inferred from the section on tin boats above, seventeen-foot center console skiffs have to be carried on trailers. Fortunately, these boats are just light enough that they, too, can be carried on simple trailers and towed with cars with relatively small engines. Portlock and I both tow our skiffs with four-cylinder, four-wheel-drive station wagons.

Shallow-water operation is enhanced greatly by a power trim and tilt system on the engine that allows you to tilt it part of the way out of the water. When you are running slowly with the engine tilted, be sure that the water intake for the cooling system is still below the surface so that the water pump can operate. If not, you run the risk of major engine damage.

Be sure to provide your boat with a push-pole as well. There will be times and places where it is indispensable. You will need at least a ten-foot pole, longer if possible. I am currently using a modified twelve-foot closet pole, which costs about one-tenth the price of a good fiberglass push-pole. It is adequate for my needs, but one day it would be nice to have a really good eighteen-foot glass pole. My skiff was built originally for the flats around the Florida Keys, and poling her can be downright pleasant.

Another mode of transportation that is useful in some areas where creeks and tidal ponds have shallow mouths is simply to climb overboard and pull the boat along by hand. Once inside, you can put the engine down or pick up the push-pole to move yourself along as appropriate.

A final advantage of center console skiffs is that they are wide open, so they do not insulate you from your surroundings. Even though the speed and noise of the engine can intrude on your observations of the world around you, under the circumstances discussed above, these powerboats can be excellent vehicles.

If it sounds as though Portlock and I are prejudiced about the boats we use for poking around, it is because we are. If you already have a boat that does not quite fit the prescriptions we have laid out, consider the points that have been raised about what makes a boat useful for exploring the Bay's tributaries, then measure your own boat's performance against them. Remember to be pragmatic. For what you are doing, the boat you already have may serve you well, at least for a time. The most important thing is to get out on the water. As you begin to get a sense of your own boat's weaknesses and strengths, you may want to change. Then we hope the guidelines above will be useful to you.

We have one last piece of advice. You may have noticed by the text above that each one of us owns more than one boat. Proliferating boats for particular purposes seems to go along with spending a few years exploring. Fortunately, all these boats are small, so that the overall investment and the annual maintenance costs are still quite low.

Experience, and How to Get It Safely

Being confident and comfortable on the water is essential to small boat exploring on the Chesapeake. Nothing sours a day more than being afraid, or miserably hot or cold. Experience brings the right measure of comfort and confidence. There is no substitute for time on the water. "You gotta pay the rent," as one of the upper Bay's best charter captains is fond of saying.

But even he started one day at a time, the same as the rest of us. Go and explore when you can. Enjoy whatever the river gives you. Sooner or later, the days accumulate and experience comes.

There *are* some ways to smooth the process. First, be cautious. Don't underestimate the Bay and its rivers. You won't find roaring white water here, but you will find winds, strong tides, deep water, soft bottoms, heat, cold, and thunderstorms. Learn how to deal with them and keep your anxiety level low.

Second, get to know your boat. You needn't be an old salt, but you should know how to handle it and take care of it. If you are new to boating, take a course.

For canoes and kayaks, the American Red Cross offers free Basic Canoeing courses that do an excellent job with fundamentals. Contact your local chapter. Make sure your instructor knows that you plan to spend time on tidal rivers. Write the Chesapeake Bay Foundation (162 Prince George Street, Annapolis, MD 21401) for a schedule of its guided weekend trips. Its field instructors are experienced and always ready to share their knowledge.

If you have an outboard skiff, learn the care and feeding of your engine. Read your owner's manual from cover to cover. If you have bought it second-hand and there is no manual, contact a dealer who sells the brand or write the company and order one. Learn to load the boat so that it trims (balances) properly and find what speeds it is happiest at. Check with the Red Cross. Some chapters offer powerboat courses. The Boating Administration of the Maryland Department of Natural Resources (Tawes State Office Building, Annapolis, MD 21401) has a good basic boating course available by mail. Write for information. Other sources of instruction (classroom only) are the U.S. Power Squadrons and the U.S. Coast Guard Auxiliary. The auxiliary also offers free courtesy examinations for boats. A courtesy exam is an excellent way to have the basic condition and safety equipment on your boat checked each year by an experienced boatman. Most newspaper outdoor and boating columns carry notifications of courses and examinations. Many marina operators and boat dealers have schedules as well. Finally, the auxiliary and the power squadrons often have exhibits at fairs and boat shows.

If you have a good rowboat, chances are you already know how to use it. There are a couple of excellent chapters on exploring in R. D. "Pete" Culler's *Boats, Oars, and Rowing* (International Marine Publishing Co.: Camden, ME, 1978).

Notice that the instructions above all involve *using* your boat. That is the only way to get comfortable with it. Here are some general guidelines.

At first, be conservative. Take short trips and stay close to home. There will be plenty to see. Most of the trips described here are short anyway, to allow plenty of time for looking, fishing, and exploring. Keep distances under two miles in a canoe, kayak, or rowboat at first, five miles in a powerboat (remember to carry plenty of gas anyway). Give yourself lots of time. Just in case, make sure someone knows where you are going and when you expect to return.

Start early and come in early to minimize the risk of a thunderstorm in spring, summer, and fall. This schedule will allow you plenty of daylight at the end of the day if you need it to deal with something unforeseen. Until you are experienced, don't go out in cold weather, especially when water temperatures are under 50°F (10°C). Hypothermia is a killer.

Check the weather. Newspapers, TV stations, and the telephone company all offer weather forecasts. Special radios to receive National Weather Service forecasts are available at low cost from most boating stores and mail-order houses. Especially avoid thunderstorms and high winds. Any wind over twelve knots is too much for the inexperienced explorer.

Know where you are going. Carry a map (see information below) and a simple hand compass. Measure distances. Keep track of where you are all the time, especially in the big salt marshes. You won't need complex orienteering and navigation skills, just some concentration.

Dress for the season. Extra clothing in cool weather and sun protection in summer are essential. In all but the hottest seasons, it is safe to assume that the weather will be 10°F cooler on the water than it is on land. Remember too that water temperature is usually lower than air temperature.

Finally, learn one thing at a time. Whatever you come home with is worth something. Be patient.

four

Natural History Gear

L ots of tools are available to help the small boat explorer learn about the water. Here are some favorites.

Eyes and Ears

Eyes and ears are the most important natural history tools to carry. Without them, all the sophisticated equipment in the world is worthless.

We're all blessed with varying combinations of visual and auditory acuity. Not everyone can pick out a soaring eagle 500 yards over a river without binoculars or identify warblers by their calls as they fly through a cypress swamp, let alone do both, but such extremes of perception are not necessary to take great joy in poking around the Bay's waterways. Seeing and hearing are also learned skills. The happiest explorers are those who teach themselves to use what they have well.

It is particularly important to learn to look and listen for details. In plants, for example, look for specific and obvious structural differences like height and shape of leaves. Any marsh tends to look like a uniform gaggle of plants until you examine it closely. It's a good first exercise to see how many species you can find in an area. Never mind what their names are or how they function in the community at this point. Try to find similarities and differences between the plants so that you can count species. By the time you are done, you will have a sense of the details of each.

Another good exercise is to look for schools of fish swimming around just under the surface of the water. Summer on brackish rivers is a good situation for practicing this skill. If you look carefully at the water's surface, you will see little cat's-paws riffles that the wind makes. Stare at the cat's-paws for several minutes until you have a sense in your mind of the patterns. Then look for other patterns on the surface that are different from the wind patterns. A school of small menhaden working just below the surface will tend to move in unison, with each fish following its neighbor in a very precise, regular pattern. That pattern will stand out against the more chaotic cat's-paws.

Many fishing guides dazzle their clients with their ability to observe fish on the surface. When asked how they recognize them, the guides reply, "Something just didn't look right." Of course, there is no right or wrong involved, but such a guide has made a study of finding a pattern that doesn't fit in with ripples caused by the movement of wind and tide. The difference in pattern attracts his/her attention and scrutiny.

Look carefully at the lay of the land around the waterway. One of the first details that you will pick up is the big looping meander bends that the tidal rivers follow. You will quickly notice a pattern in which the river or creek scoops out mud, sand, and gravel on the outside of the bend, forming a deep hole with a high bank and woods, while on the inside of the curve, where the current slows down, sediment settles out, forming large marshes. It's obvious in these places that there is a very close relationship between the lay of the land and the way the waterway works.

Sometimes, the lay of the land can give you a clue as to how well the waterway has been treated by the people who live around it. In general, steep banks on the sides of a creek mean deep water in the channel. In some creeks, however, especially on the upper western shore of the Bay in rivers like the Severn and the South, creeks with high banks turn out to be very shallow because poor sediment-control practices during road and house construction have allowed silt to run downstream into the headwaters. Some of these creeks were indeed six to eight feet deep a century ago and now have less than a foot of water at low tide.

Spend part of each trip listening carefully to the sounds of birds and fish. This is relatively easy to do in a canoe or other self-propelled boat, although even then it is also possible to let one's mind wander and forget to listen. In powerboats it is important to concentrate on looking and listening at least part of the time. Ospreys, red-tailed hawks, herons, and geese are often quite vocal. In time, you will develop a sort of "peripheral listening" that helps you hear birds like these as they fly overhead.

Spend part of your time staring at the sky too. Scan it to look for silent soaring birds, like eagles, hawks, and turkey vultures. Scan the surface of the water with binoculars too. Looking at some of the upper Bay's rivers in the fall of the year can turn up flocks of loons, for example. These birds are often very quiet when they are feeding, and you will not notice them unless you look for them.

Finally, keep an ear out for fish. From time to time, species like menhaden, carp, bluefish, and rockfish (striped bass) will break the surface. Having an ear tuned to that kind of sound may not help you to see the fish itself, but you can turn and see where it was. Tuning in does enhance your chances of actually seeing one roll.

At first it is difficult to absorb details and fit them together. Just keep looking. As described above, a friend once told me that the way to study a painting in a museum is to stare at it until you get bored and then look at it for ten more minutes. I find that technique works amazingly well.

As you work to see details, you will find that you begin to notice them more readily. Some will suddenly stand out. Then you'll realize that you're beginning to see patterns, like the way a school of menhaden differs from a wind ripple, or the difference between a turkey vulture and an eagle as they soar, or the similarities between high banks on meander curves from one creek to another, or the different plant communities on a high marsh and a low marsh.

Keep cultivating these skills. Noticing details and sensing patterns are extremely valuable in learning to see and hear what is around you on the Bay and its tributaries.

Aids to Sight and Hearing

Athough eyes and ears are the primary tools for the small boat explorer, a number of useful tools can enhance what we find out about a waterway. A good pair of binoculars is an obvious choice. These instruments are a subculture in themselves. There are all kinds of opinions about which glasses are more efficient, ranging from the fact that 7×50 glasses gather light well, so that they are very effective at dawn and dusk, to the fact that top-quality 6×35 glasses are very light and can be carried easily. A good case can be made for rubber-armored waterproof glasses when you're paddling a canoe. I have an old pair of 6×30 waterproof glasses which I use for the best of reasons: they were given to me. A serious birder would want a better pair, but for my kind of general use, these are satisfactory.

Another top choice is a good set of field guides. In a small boat, there is no point in overburdening yourself, but three volumes are adequate to cover over 90 percent of what you will see. A number are listed in the

"Books" section below. I recommend a general field guide to the Bay and its creatures, a good bird guide, and a good marsh plant guide as a starter set.

Underwater Equipment

So far, all the gear listed is designed to help you see and recognize things above the water's surface. Most of the Bay's waters are cloudy, making it difficult to peer into them and see clearly. In some cases, however, this is possible. It is a good learning experience simply to lie down on a dock and search carefully for activity around its pilings. In general, though, we must resort to electronics and harvest tools to learn more.

Nets

Nets can be extremely useful. Two kinds that the small boat explorer can carry easily are a minnow seine and a cast net. Both are readily available from sporting goods stores and mail-order catalogs. A twenty-five-foot minnow seine set on two closet poles is an excellent device for catching bait and for sampling small fish. On tidal fresh rivers in the summertime, it may well turn up as many as fifteen different species in a single pull, as noted above.

A minnow seine is a fine-mesh net with floats on the top line and lead weights along the bottom. Two people walk parallel to the shore with the net, holding its base on the bottom with the poles. At a predetermined point, the inshore person stops and the person in deeper water swings the net around onto the bank, where it can be pulled up and its contents examined. Be careful. A seine can catch a lot of fish, and the small ones can die if they are handled roughly. It is best to cull (sort) the contents of the net over the water, rather than high and dry on shore.

The cast net is a round net designed to be thrown. Its design is at least 2,000 years old. When thrown out flat onto the water like a big Frisbee, the net sinks quickly to the bottom by virtue of a series of lead weights around its circumference. Brail lines tied to the outer edges of the net lead back through a round thimble at the center to a swivel which is tied to a twenty-five-foot main line that is looped around the thrower's wrist. Once the net has sunk to the bottom, pulling on the main line causes the brail lines to gather the net up into a mushroom shape, with the catch in the outer folds.

Rumor has it that learning to throw a cast net takes at least five years. The rumor is false—most people can learn to throw a four-foot (radius) net in three to five throws. Ask for instructions when you buy your net.

Pulling a minnow seine on the north side of the Big Salt Marsh at Poquoson. This net is a basic tool for anyone exploring the Chesapeake's rivers, creeks, and marshes. Photo by Bill Portlock.

There are refinements, like learning to make long throws accurately over moving schools of fish, but 'most anyone can pick up a small net, fool around with it for fifteen minutes, and catch a few fish. Then the refinements come with more experience.

Cast nets are particularly useful for catching bait like menhaden that show close to the surface, but they can also be thrown into holes five to fifteen feet deep where they may catch fish up to ten pounds. It sounds as though letting a cast net drop into a hole is like shooting fish in a barrel, but the truth is that the amount of bottom covered by such a net is relatively small. You won't catch much by throwing one this way until you figure out where in the hole the fish are most likely to be. Then the results may surprise you.

Another very useful piece of gear is a roller net. This device is a long wooden handle attached to a rectangular frame eighteen by eight inches or twenty-eight by twelve inches. From the frame hangs a fine-mesh net, but attached to the leading edge of the frame is a wooden roller which turns on shafts fixed to the two front corners. Roller nets are much more readily available in Maryland than they are in Virginia, but they are also relatively easy to make. They have been used for years both to harvest soft crabs from grass beds and to catch grass shrimp for bait.

One fishes a roller net by pushing it along so that the roller turns on the bottom. As might be expected, working one of these across a mud flat or through a grass bed will catch shrimp, soft crabs, small fish, and a number of other creatures. If you don't have a roller net, run a crab net with a fine-mesh bag in it through a grass bed and catch some of these creatures. Of course, a minnow seine will do the same. The major advantages of the roller net are that it can be used in tight spaces and that only one person is needed to manipulate it.

Fishing Tackle

Fishing tackle is always useful. When I was running canoe trips for CBF, I carried a light spinning rod and a box full of small plastic-tailed jigs. I fished for whatever turned up, rather than for any specific species, and the variety was always interesting. I caught white perch, yellow perch, sunfish, crappie, largemouth bass, small bluefish, channel and white catfish, chain pickerel, and rockfish. Between the rod and the cast net, it was a rare day that I didn't come home with something to eat. Fishing is a whole other story, but a rod and reel can be a good tool for analyzing a waterway, and the fresh seafood that results deepens the experience by making the angler physically a part of the waterway's food web.

Depth-Sounder

In almost any small boat, a simple depth-sounder is an excellent tool for seeing what would otherwise be invisible. Flashing depth-sounders and liquid crystal display units can both be bought as portables. Spend a little time with the instruction book and talk to the dealer or manufacturer if necessary. You should find that within a day of actually using the device, you have learned to spot fish, to read what kind of bottom you are over, and to get a sense of the shape of the waterway's basin. Then watch it consistently, and you will find that patterns begin to show up. A depth-sounder will broaden your horizons 100 percent. More than any other device, it will keep you from being totally surface-oriented and help you "see" what is beneath you. You will miss a lot without one. Incidentally, a suction-mount portable transducer works well on canoes and aluminum skiffs.

Other Bait-Catching Tools

Other bait-catching gear can be very useful. Crab lines, nets, and pots catch crabs. The nets and pots sometimes catch other creatures as well. A shovel can be a very useful tool for analyzing mud flats and sandbars, particularly on tidal rivers. Make a square box by nailing pieces of pressure-treated 2×4s together and then attach screen wire across the bottom. Reinforce the bottom by nailing large-mesh hardware cloth over it. You now have a sieve box that will allow you to sort through bottom sediments that you dig up with the shovel. Depending on where you are, a broad variety of worms, shellfish, and crustaceans will turn up on the screen. You may be able to use some for fish bait. Others will simply give you insight into the waterway.

Salinity Indicators

It is useful to know the salinity of the water. Small chemical kits are available for about $30 from the LaMotte Chemical Products Company (Chestertown, MD 21620). Short of buying one and maintaining it, you may be able to get a sense of salinity both directly and indirectly with your own senses. First, it is possible to taste the water and see how salty it is. (Be sure to spit the water out after you have tasted it, and rinse your mouth. Most of the Bay is not fit to drink.) Most Bay scientists and CBF field guides can taste water and figure the salinity with an accuracy of 3 to 5 parts per thousand. You may start off with categories like very salty, salty, mildly salty, and fresh. Either way, salt is a major determinant of plant communities, as we have noted above, and having a sense of it is useful.

A second way to estimate the salinity is by looking at the plant community. Species composition in any one area is a good reflection of the average salinity over the course of a year there. If you read Chapter 2 on characteristics of waterways, you'll get a sense of how to use the plant community to estimate salinity.

Scientists use more sophisticated gear, like dissolved oxygen meters, conductivity meters (for salinity), spectrophotometers, traps, and trawl nets, to tell them what's going on underwater. Don't feel intimidated by the idea of equipment. Keep your own kit simple and learn to use it well; it will teach you more than you can imagine. Don't get more complicated than you need. And learn to look—your own senses are the best tools you have.

Maps and Charts

Good maps and charts are essential tools. Don't go exploring without them. You need to know where you are going, and you will find that a good chart will help you understand the waterway you are on. Many of the best access points are on back roads, so you will need highway maps with good detail as well. The following are some basics:

Chartbooks

Several sources produce chartbooks. The most comprehensive one is *ADC's Waterproof Chartbook of the Chesapeake Bay*, available from most fishing tackle shops and marinas or from ADC, 6440 General Green Way, Alexandria, VA 22312 or call 1-800-ADC-MAPS. Detail of both waterways and roads is excellent, though coverage of the upper tidal rivers in Maryland is not complete. Still, if you plan to carry only one chartbook, this is it. This chartbook also carries an extensive list of commercial marinas and launch ramps.

The official source for navigation charts is the National Ocean Service, Riverdale, MD 20737-1199 (301-713-3074). Individual charts of specific waterways in several levels of detail are available directly from NOS or from its authorized agents (generally large marine supply stores). Those agents and the ADC *Chartbook* have an index for all the NOS charts of the Chesapeake Bay region.

Access Guides

The Maryland Department of Natural Resources and the Virginia Department of Game and Inland Fisheries publish excellent guides to their states' public landings, *A Fisherman's Guide to Maryland Piers and Boat Ramps* and the *Virginia Boating Guide*. Both are available from regional centers that handle boating registrations. You can also call 1-800-688-FINS (MD) or 804-367-1000 (VA) to ask to have a copy mailed to you. Finally, you can visit the agencies' web sites to get the information directly:

Maryland—http://www.dnr.state.md.us/fisheries

Virginia—http://www.dgif.state.va.us/boating/public boating access

Both guides are full of information. Some Maryland counties require boaters to purchase permits for use of their public landings. The permits are bargains ($10-15/year, available at local fishing tackle shops), and the funds help the counties maintain the facilities. The Maryland guide notes which counties require these permits.

Contour Maps

For details of creeks, secondary roads, and land countours, use the fine-scale topographic maps published by the U.S. Geological Survey (USGS). They are sold by most outdoor stores that cater to backpackers, or they can be ordered directly from USGS, Reston, VA 22092. Write first for an index and ordering information.

In addition, the Maryland Geological Survey publishes large and detailed maps of all the state's counties. While not as detailed as USGS topo maps, these can be very useful in upriver areas. Call the Maryland Geological Survey in Baltimore (410-554-5505) for information.

Road Maps

Finally, the Department of Transportation in each state produces an excellent official and free-of-charge state road map with good detail of roads (though still not as complete as USGS topo maps). In Virginia, write the Division of Administrative Services, 1401 E. Broad Street, Richmond, VA 23319. In Maryland, write the State Highway Administration, Baltimore, MD 21203.

The educational value of a map varies inversely with its ease of handling in a small boat. It is difficult, for example, to work with a series of topo maps or a large Maryland county map in a canoe or small aluminum skiff. Thus, something that is waterproof and easily handled, like the ADC *Chartbook*, is of great value. You will find, however, that topo and county maps can be excellent reference works to scope out a trip itinerary ahead of time. Use them to do some homework and write notes on your chartbook. Time invested in preparation can pay big dividends out on the water.

Books

This list is not meant to be comprehensive. It includes the books I have found to be most useful over the years.

Field Guides

Gibbons, Euell, *Stalking the Blue-Eyed Scallop*, David McKay Co.: New York, 1963.

———, *Stalking the Wild Asparagus*, David McKay Co.: New York, 1961.

> Two classic books on foraging wild foods. Euell Gibbons loved the Chesapeake Bay region, and that feeling shines through in his books.

Lippson, A. J., and R. L., *Life in the Chesapeake Bay*, Johns Hopkins University Press: Baltimore, 1997.

> A comprehensive, illustrated guide to fish, invertebrates, and plants found around the Chesapeake. The information is organized around certain communities: sand beaches, inland bays, freshwater marshes, saltwater marshes, and oyster rocks. Highly recommended.

McClane, A. J., *A Guide to the Freshwater Fishes of North America*, Holt, Rinehart, & Winston: New York, 1974.

———, *A Guide to the Saltwater Fishes of North America*, Holt, Rinehart, & Winston: New York, 1975.

> The two McClane's guides are excellent for detailed study of the fishes that you will encounter while exploring the Chesapeake and its tributaries.

Penrod, Ken, *Fishing the Tidal Potomac River*, PPC Publishing: Beltsville, MD, 1989.

———, *Tidewater Bass Fishing*, PPC Publishing: Beltsville, MD, 1991.

> Ken Penrod is a most experienced and expert fishing guide who has put in several thousand days on the water over the past ten years, fishing mostly but not exclusively for largemouth bass. These books contain detailed information on the Bay's rivers. Highly recommended for fishermen.

Robbins, Chandler S., Bertel Bruun, and Herbert S. Zim, *Birds of North America*, Golden Press: New York, 1966.

> There are plenty of other bird guides, but over the years, this one has proven to be the most consistently useful to me. Highly recommended.

Silberhorn, Gene M., *Common Marsh Plants of the Mid-Atlantic Coast*, Johns Hopkins University Press: Baltimore, 1982.

This field guide is essential for identifying fresh- and saltwater marsh plants as well as beach species. It is the very best available. Highly recommended.

White, Christopher P., *Chesapeake Bay: Nature of the Estuary, A Field Guide*, Tidewater Publishers: Centreville, MD, 1989.

Another excellent Chesapeake field guide with extensive descriptions of a great variety of plants and animals, plus discussions of various biological communities. Highly recommended.

Natural History

Environmental Protection Agency, *Chesapeake Bay: Introduction to an Ecosystem*, 1982. Available postpaid for $2.00 from the Chesapeake Bay Foundation, 162 Prince George Street, Annapolis, MD 21401.

An invaluable primer about basic Bay ecology and environmental problems. Highly recommended.

Frye, John, *The Men All Singing: The Story of Menhaden Fishing*, The Donning Company: Virginia Beach, 1978.

A comprehensive and fascinating history of menhaden fishing on the Atlantic and Gulf coasts, including excellent material on the natural history of this most important denizen of the Chesapeake community.

Horton, Tom, *Bay Country*, Johns Hopkins University Press: Baltimore, 1988.

A lucid and literate discussion of the Chesapeake Bay/Susquehanna River system, including the problems it faces and its many values as a natural resource for the people of the region. Highly recommended.

Horton, Tom, and Wm. E. Eichbaum, *Turning the Tide: Saving the Chesapeake Bay*, Island Press: Washington, DC, 1991.

A comprehensive look at the state of the Chesapeake Bay written for the Chesapeake Bay Foundation by two discerning observers, with detailed accounts of progress and remaining problem areas, plus recommendations for further improvement. Highly recommended.

Meanley, Brooke, *Birds and Marshes of the Chesapeake Bay Country*, Tidewater Publishers: Centreville, MD, 1975.

An interesting collection of stories about Bay birds and marshes. Written by a retired field biologist from the U.S. Fish and Wildlife Service, it provides an important perspective on marshes as bird habitat.

Schubel, Jerry, *The Living Chesapeake*, Johns Hopkins University Press: Baltimore, 1982.

A collection of essays and photographs with wonderful pieces on the Bay's geologic history, its marshes, and the estuarine animals that use the Bay in different ways: oysters, water fleas, blue crabs, and striped bass. It is an important book especially because of its geological point of view.

Warner, William W., *Beautiful Swimmers: Watermen, Crabs, and the Chesapeake Bay*, Atlantic-Little, Brown: Boston, 1976.

The classic book about the Chesapeake's blue crab and the people who fish for it commercially. A Pulitzer Prize winner, beautifully researched and written. Most highly recommended.

Williams, John Page. *Chesapeake Almanac,* Tidewater Publishers: Centreville, MD, 1993.

A collection of sketches of Chesapeake natural history, organized around the seasons.

History

These books offer good perspective on the way things used to be on the Chesapeake. Think about how the Bay's natural resources have influenced our history in the region.

Burgess, Robert F., *Steamboats Out of Baltimore*, Tidewater Publishers: Centreville, MD, 1968.

The Chesapeake Bay steamboat era is a rich period of history for the rivers. The schedules of the old steamers indicating the numerous stops and trips are particularly interesting. The pictures do justice to these beautiful craft.

———, *This Was Chesapeake Bay,* Tidewater Publishers: Centreville, MD, 1963.

A useful overview of Bay history from the Indian cultures to amusement parks at Tolchester. It chronicles the development of maritime activities from the logwood trade to cruises down the Bay from Baltimore.

———, *Chesapeake Circle*, Tidewater Publishers: Centreville, MD, 1964.

A sequel to *This Was Chesapeake Bay*, with many sketches of old Bay sailing craft, from schooners to skipjacks.

Keith, Robert C., *Baltimore Harbor*, Ocean World Publishing: Baltimore, 1981. (Now available from the Johns Hopkins University Press, Baltimore)

A highly readable account of the development of Baltimore Harbor and its present-day activities.

Middleton, Arthur Pierce, *Tobacco Coast*, Johns Hopkins University Press: Baltimore, 1984.

A reissued comprehensive history of the Chesapeake during the colonial period. Originally printed in 1954, it was the first book to treat the Bay as one region, with the fortunes of both Virginia and Maryland linked to their common resource. Long, but well worth the effort.

Tilp, Frederick, *The Chesapeake Bay of Yore. Mainly about the Rowing and Sailing Craft.*

The title tells all, except that the book has beautiful line drawings.

————, *This was Potomac River.*

A labor of love. Tilp sailed the tidal Potomac for forty years from the early 1930s till the mid '70s and knew it well, all of it. He provides an incomparable picture of creeks, fish, boats, and life on the river over the past two centuries.

The two books by Frederick Tilp are out of print, but may be available in libraries.

Traditional Cruise Guides

These books have all been written for deep-draft cruising power- and sailboats, so they deal with the Bay itself and the lower rivers. Even so, they can be useful resources in those areas, and they contain good material on weather, places to visit, and commercial marinas.

Blanchard, F. S., W. E. Stone, and A. M. Hays, *A Cruising Guide to the Chesapeake*, Dodd, Mead, and Company: New York, 1988.

This is the standard, first published in 1950 and revised several times since then. It provides excellent information on most of the Bay's cruising areas.

Guide to Cruising the Chesapeake Bay, published by *Chesapeake Bay Magazine*, 1819 Bay Ridge Avenue, Annapolis, MD 21403.

Magazine staff members revise this cruise guide every year, so it contains a great deal of fresh, firsthand information from them, and various of their friends.

Shellenberger, William H., *Cruising the Chesapeake: A Gunkholer's Guide*, International Marine Publishing Co.: Camden, ME, 1990.

Shellenberger's guide is a good one for exploring creeks and coves of the lower rivers and the Bay. He places more emphasis than others on areas to explore by dinghy.

Magnificent fisherman—the great blue heron. Photo by Bill Portlock.

Part Two

TRIP SUGGESTIONS

For all the time that Bill Portlock, Janet Harvey, and I have spent exploring the Chesapeake's rivers and marshes in canoes and outboard skiffs, there is still quite a lot that we haven't yet seen. Even creeks we feel we know well change from season to season and from year to year. Hence there is a joy of discovery in virtually every trip that any one of us takes. We wish you the same.

What follows is a series of broad trip suggestions, with a few more specific trip descriptions to help you begin poking around. We won't—and can't—tell you everything you'll find. You're your own explorer, and your own discoverer.

There is enough material in the general waterway and season description chapters to give you a head start on patterns to look for. These trip suggestions will give you some general areas and access points on each river system that we feel are good ones for small boat exploring, and we'll go into a little more detail on some of our favorite sites.

Please be careful about the access points you choose. Be patient and respect the rights of property owners. At the outset, we recommend that you work from public landings, unless you have clear permission from the owners of private ones. As you spend time on the Bay's waterways, you may well meet some river people and accumulate a repertoire of private access points as we have, but begin with well-built and well-maintained landings that are open to the public. The best sources of information on them are Maryland's *A Fishermans' Guide to Maryland Piers and Boat Ramps* and the *Virginia Boating Guide* (see p. 86–7).

The yellow pages of regional telephone books, ADC's *Chartbook of the Chesapeake Bay*, and the *Chesapeake Bay Magazine*'s current *Guide to Cruising the Chesapeake Bay* can give you the names of a number of commercial marinas, especially on the lower portions of the rivers. See the section on maps in Chapter 4 for more information on these publications.

Beyond these general directions and our suggestions for keeping yourself safe, you're on your own. May the joys of discovery be yours.

five

Upper Eastern Shore

Northeast, Elk, Bohemia, Sassafras, and Chester Rivers

Theoretically, the Eastern Shore begins on the Cecil County side of the Susquehanna. The river is tidal from just above Port Deposit down to Perryville, at the river's mouth. The Susquehanna and the vast complex of the Susquehanna Flats will be covered in a later chapter.

The section from Perryville up into the Northeast River to the town of Northeast and around to Turkey Point at the mouth of the Elk is an extension of the Susquehanna Flats, with broad expanses of shallow water. This area is much more suitable for outboard skiffs and sea kayaks than it is for canoes or rowboats. If operating a powerboat, be very careful of partially or completely submerged tree stumps out on the flats. Furnace Bay, just east of Perryville, is worth exploring, as is the town of Northeast, which has a nice little community museum in its waterfront park devoted to waterfowling and fishing on the flats. The Northeast River itself offers good variety to fishermen, including especially large-mouth bass, catfish, crappie, yellow perch, and white perch.

The best launch ramp for this area is at Elk Neck State Park on Turkey Point (410-287-5333). This park is an excellent public facility, offering boat rentals, campgrounds, and rental cabins in addition to the ramp. Be sure to call for information; in some years, it is closed in the off-season.

The land in this part of the Bay country is very different from the rest of the Eastern Shore: It has high elevation, up to 300 feet on Elk Neck, which makes that land look almost like a mountain range from the flats or the Elk River.

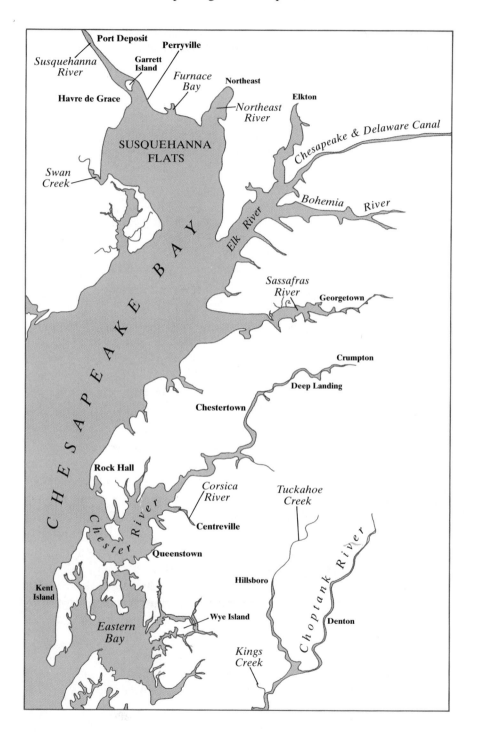

Port Deposit
Perryville
Susquehanna
River
Garrett
Island
Furnace
Bay
Northeast
Havre de Grace
Elkton
Northeast
River
SUSQUEHANNA
FLATS
Chesapeake & Delaware Canal
Swan
Creek
Bohemia   River
Elk River
Sassafras
River
Georgetown
CHESAPEAKE BAY
Crumpton
Deep Landing
Chestertown
Rock Hall
Corsica
River
Tuckahoe
Creek
Chester River
Centreville
Queenstown
Hillsboro
Choptank River
Kent
Island
Wye Island
Denton
Eastern
Bay
Kings
Creek

The soil from the Elk east and south is very fertile, and like other areas of the Bay, it was settled early, in the mid-seventeenth century. The rolling topography drains to streams that could be dammed for mills. Combined with plenty of navigable waterways, these conditions provided the whole upper Eastern Shore with an excellent opportunity to grow grains, grind them to flour, and ship them to Europe. After the Revolution, this area was the breadbasket for our young nation, so shipping was still important, but the grain stayed on the Atlantic Coast. The area is still largely agricultural today.

Virtually all the waterways in this section are tidal fresh, except for the mouth of the Chester. Historically, the area grew vast marshes of mixed freshwater vegetation and lush beds of submerged aquatic vegetation like wild celery and pondweeds. Although the submerged vegetation has been damaged in recent years, some of it is still around, and so are the marshes. Thus the area has always been blessed with birdlife. As recently as a hundred years ago, waterfowl were so numerous they were said to "darken the skies." The numbers are down now, as they are everywhere in North America, but fall and winter are still great times for the birds, especially Canada geese.

These waterways also grow large fish populations. The complex of rivers and the Chesapeake and Delaware Canal on the Elk form the richest rockfish spawning ground on the Atlantic Coast, with adults coming up to spawn in April and May, and juveniles spending the first two years of their lives in the area. The rockfish's close cousin, the white perch, is also abundant here, as are catfish, yellow perch, and largemouth bass.

Channel catfish are now the most important commercial finfish in Maryland (1.4 million pounds in 1989), most of them caught in hoop traps and shipped live to fish-for-pay ponds in the Midwest. If you are prowling around one of these rivers in the summertime and see a deadrise workboat with a large live tank in its cockpit, you can pretty well assume that it is a catfish boat.

Watermen in this area are experts not only at catching what is available, but also at marketing their catch. In addition to catfish, they are adept at handling white perch, yellow perch, carp, eels, and even snapping turtles. Surprisingly, there are also plenty of crabs in this area, and several watermen run exceptionally large strings of pots.

In years past, shad were also extremely important in this area during their runs in April, May, and June. In the early part of the twentieth century, they were Maryland's most lucrative commercial species. Anyone who has ever developed a taste for shad and shad roe or who has caught one of these wonderful fish on a hook and line hopes that present efforts to restore them will be successful by the turn of the century.

The public launch ramp at Elk Neck State Park is well positioned for exploring the Elk and Bohemia rivers. This is wide water, better suited to skiffs than to paddle/oar craft.

None of us has been in the Bohemia, but we hear that it is beautiful. It was settled and named early by Augustine Hermann, a native of Bohemia (now part of Czechoslovakia) who acquired his land at Bohemia Manor in the late seventeenth century in exchange for compiling and drawing one of the early maps of the Chesapeake region. It was a fine map, and Hermann put together a grand estate.

The Sassafras is also a beautiful river, with high wooded banks. If you are shrewd as you explore it, you may be able to pick out the sites of some of the old farm wharves by looking for the gullies where the roads ran down to the water. The river is very popular for cruising boats, with good anchorages and fresh water for swimming (that means no sea nettles in late summer). Largemouth bass fishing is good throughout the river (see Ken Penrod's book for details). There are large marinas as far up as the Rt. 213 bridge that crosses the river between Georgetown and Fredericktown, but above the bridge, there is very little boat traffic.

Lloyd Creek and Turner Creek, just east of Betterton, are good small boat waters. Use the ramps at Turner Creek Park (410-778-1948) or at Betterton Beach Waterfront Park (410-778-1948).

The public landings at Fredericktown and Georgetown provide good access to the upper part of the river for small boats. Call Cecil County (410-658-3000) for information on the Fredericktown landing and Kent County (410-778-7439) for information on the Gregg Neck Public Landing near Georgetown. About five miles upriver, there is a dirt ramp at Foxhole Public Landing which is at the end of Fox Hole Road, off Rt. 290, a quarter-mile from its intersection with Rt. 301.

Fox Hole Landing is a lovely, quiet spot, with a creek just across the river fed by a farmer's millpond. Just upstream is an unusual stand of large hemlock trees, beyond which the Sassafras narrows down to a tiny stream between tidal fresh marshes. In a canoe or kayak, it is possible to paddle up past Rt. 301 to a point where the creek forks. In the seventeenth and early eighteenth centuries, there was a town here, appropriately named Sassafras. If you have paddled up this far, you will have noticed that the river has silted in considerably from nearly three centuries of land clearing and farm runoff, which undoubtedly contributed to the demise of the town. Nonetheless, the head of the Sassafras River is an attractive and uncrowded waterway.

Below the Sassafras, Fairlee Creek offers protected waters for exploring, and it has a landing on it. Call Kent County (410-778-7439) for information. This is a major cruising boat harbor, so we will leave a description of it to the cruise guides.

Below Fairlee Creek is Rock Hall harbor, which primarily serves watermen and cruising boats. The next complex of water for small boats is the Chester River, and a valuable one it is.

The Chester is one of the Eastern Shore's major rivers, stretching from its mouth between Eastern Neck Island and Kent Island all the way across the upper Shore even into Delaware. Its lower reaches are brackish, its upper reaches tidal fresh. Its fertile soil, deep creeks and coves, and twenty-five miles of main river channel ensured extensive settlement early in the history of the Maryland colony, during the seventeenth century. Eastern Neck Island was the home of the Wickes family for some 300 years, and they kept the island busy. One creek on the east side winds back into a marsh and stops. It is Shipyard Creek, and it was an active place in the seventeenth and eighteenth centuries, but there is no trace there today of its former trade.

Eastern Neck Island is now a national wildlife refuge, with walking trails and a boat ramp at Bogles Wharf. Call the refuge office (410-639-7056) for information about access. Bogles Wharf is operated by Kent County (410-778-7439). Eastern Neck is a good area to explore in any kind of a small boat, but the mouth of the Chester is quite broad, so paddle/oar craft would do well to stay close to the island itself. Shipyard Creek is a good destination for a short trip. It is just below Bogles Wharf.

Three miles north of Bogles Wharf is Grays Inn Creek, the site of a very early town, New Yarmouth, which was an important commercial center beginning about 1650. It was in fact the Kent County seat, with a courthouse and two shipyards. New Yarmouth continued as such until 1698, when the courthouse was moved upriver to Chestertown. Then it gradually disappeared.

Across the river on the Queen Anne's side is Reed Creek, which has a dirt boat ramp. Call Queen Anne's County (410-758-0835) for information. Reed is a popular stop for cruising boats, but it is also a beautiful protected waterway for exploration by small boat.

A little farther upriver is the Corsica River, with Centreville, the Queen Anne's County seat, at its head of navigation. Centreville Wharf has a paved county boat ramp (410-758-0835). The Corsica is a pretty river, with tidal fresh marshes above the bridge at the landing and brackish waters below. The upper stream is quite shallow and narrow, best suited to canoes. It is a delightful, forgotten little waterway that does not see much traffic. The marshes are full of wild rice, Walters millet, and other seed-bearing plants. For some years, I ran field trips for Centreville Middle School during the third week of September, just after the rice and millet ripened, and there was always a nice flock of blue-winged teal that had stopped their migration to feed.

Like the head of the Sassafras and most other Eastern Shore rivers, the Corsica has eaten a great deal of silt over the years, so it is quite shallow from the boat ramp upstream, but two hundred years ago, it was a port town. The old brick houses by the wharf are referred to locally as the Captains' Houses, since they were built by the men who ran the sailing vessels based there.

Below Centreville, the Corsica winds between large estates as it makes it way to the Chester. It is well worth exploring, but there is no other public landing on it, so anyone in a canoe or kayak should plan on leaving from and returning to Centreville Wharf. If you are in a power-boat, notice the red marker at the end of the long bar called Jacobs Nose, which extends from the shore at Gunston School. The channel is far over on the north bank. Over the years, many boat owners have misread this buoy to their great embarrassment.

Upriver from the Corsica is Southeast Creek, which has a dirt ramp (410-758-0835) at the end of Southeast Creek Road, off Rt. 213 just south of Church Hill. None of us has explored Southeast Creek, but we are told that is a very pretty waterway, and a reliable friend has fished its headwaters extensively for bass, perch, crappie, and catfish.

As noted above, Chestertown became the county seat in 1698 and has been the focal point for the river ever since. Early on, it was an important and prosperous port city, shipping wheat to Europe as well as up and down the Atlantic Coast. No matter what kind of boat you are in, Chestertown is worth a visit for a meal and a walk up and down its attractive streets. We will leave further details of it to the cruise guides.

Above Chestertown, the Chester is a pastoral river with several side branches coming down from the rolling land around it. These side branches and the headwaters were harnessed early on for waterpower to grind the grains that all the surrounding farms produced. The town at the river's headwaters, in fact, is named Millington for this reason. Because of the river's early and lasting commercial importance, there are old landings nearly all the way to Millington. Part of this section provides the itinerary for the trip description below.

Trip Description:
Chester River, Crumpton to Deep Landing

Type of Waterway—Tidal fresh

Directions and Access—Crumpton is on Maryland Rt. 290 approximately four miles north of that road's exit from U.S. Rt. 301. There is a ramp at the foot of First Street. Deep Landing is a Queen Anne's County wharf (410-758-0835) at the end of Deep Landing Road, off Maryland Rt. 544 about three miles west of Crumpton.

Trip Routes—Either point can be used alone for access, but if you have two cars, it is easy to set up a shuttle between them. If you do use a shuttle, choose your itinerary so that you go with the wind and the tide. If you must pick one or the other, go with the wind. It is, for example, much easier on a strong northwest wind in the fall to paddle a canoe from Deep Landing to Crumpton than vice versa, even against a falling tide.

Cautions—The basin for this part of the river is unusually wide and shallow, but there is a deep channel that snakes its way through it. No matter which direction you are travelling, you will notice very quickly that the channel is buoyed by the U.S. Coast Guard. Pay close attention to those buoys if you wish to stay in the channel, especially if you are running a powerboat. You will be surprised, for example, at the first channel marker below the Crumpton bridge. It is close to the Kent County shoreline, but it is placed correctly. The channel swings in very near to the bank there. If your powerboat is equipped with a push-pole and you don't mind running gently aground, by all means go where you want, but do so carefully. Notice too that the width of the waterway here can expose canoes, kayaks, and row craft to considerable wind. Large seas do not build up, but you may find that controlling your boat takes a lot of work in any wind over ten knots.

Comments—For most of the steamboat lines, Crumpton was the last stop. The boats ran up there and then turned around to go back down. The town was very busy in those times, since it was a major shipping point for grain and flour from the surrounding area. When the steamboats quit running in the early thirties, Crumpton declined dramatically, so that today it is simply a sleepy little town next to a river. The only major industry it can claim now is Dixon's Furniture Auction at the intersection of Rts. 290 and 544. If you are around on a Wednesday afternoon, the auction is quite a spectacle.

Other days, you can find your excitement on the river. There are several large tidal freshwater marshes along the shore, and you will find an extensive marsh on Chase Island in the middle of the river a mile below Crumpton. There are also several nice side creeks to explore. In the fall, there will be waterfowl around, and the river has the usual complement of white perch, catfish, chain pickerel, and largemouth bass if you are so inclined.

The trip is easy in paddle/oar craft. If you are in a powerboat, take advantage of your extra speed to explore the river both above Crumpton and down to Chestertown. A mile above Crumpton, the river narrows down considerably, so be careful from there up. If you run down toward Chestertown, be sure to explore Morgan Creek, about four miles below Deep Landing on the Kent County side.

six

Middle Eastern Shore

Wye and Choptank Rivers

The Wye and the Choptank are quite different from one another. The Wye is a short, winding complex of pastoral brackish waterways with beautiful old farms and estates along its banks. The Choptank, on the other hand, is the longest river on the Eastern Shore, rising in western Delaware and flowing some seventy miles to the Chesapeake. It has a long salinity gradient, with miles of tidal fresh water above its brackish lower reaches. Both rivers offer good areas for exploration by canoes, kayaks, rowing boats, and powerboats.

The two put-ins available on the Wye are Wye Landing, at the end of Wye Landing Lane, off Rt. 662 just south of Wye Mills, and Skipton Landing, on Skipton Landing Road just west of Rt. 50 and south of Wye Mills. Both are Talbot County landings. Call 410-822-2955 for information.

Just inside Bennett Point, the Wye system splits off from the Miles into two rivers—the Wye and the Wye East, which go north and east, respectively. They are connected again several miles to the north by Wye Narrows, thus forming Wye Island (see a chart). The island is a beautiful complex of old farmland and mature hardwoods, now under state ownership as a wildlife management area. Call 410-827-7577 for information.

The Wye was settled early by Europeans, especially the Lloyd family, whose first member began farming on it in the late 1600s and built a fortune from tobacco and trade. The original estate on the Wye

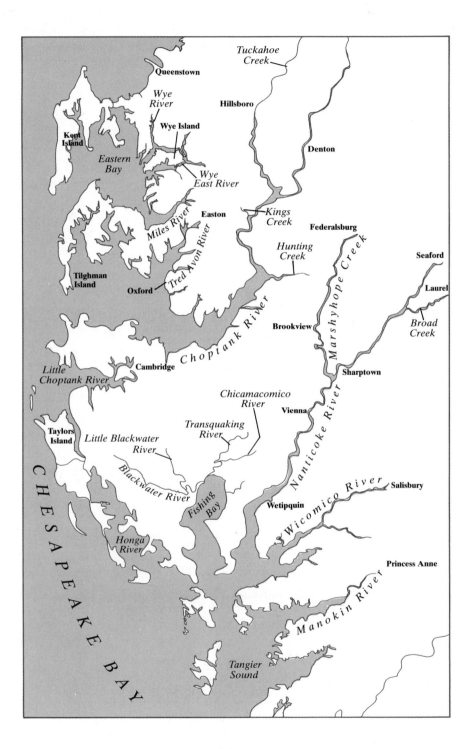

East stayed in the family's hands for 300 years. The Lloyds attracted other families to the river as well, giving rise to the rest of the estates on the Wye East and the Narrows.

The town of York once stood on Skipton Creek, just east of its confluence with the Wye East and the Narrows. York was the original Talbot County seat, with a courthouse and a jail, but little remains of it today. In the mid-1800s, Wye Island had a bustling village that was a model of division of labor and self-sufficiency. It too is gone.

Today, the most activity you will see on the river is cruising yachtsmen and watermen running trotlines for crabs. Shaw Bay, at the mouth of the Wye East, and the deep-water creeks and coves throughout the system are much-favored anchorages for cruising people. As to the trotliners, the Wye consistently gives them some of the largest jimmy crabs in the whole Chesapeake system. You'll notice a number of special trotline workboats tied up at Wye Landing.

If you go through the Narrows to the Wye, you will find that much of the land on that river has been subdivided into two- to five-acre lots, each having its own lawn and dock. This building pattern occurred in the 1970s and early '80s. The houses are nice enough, but this spread-out kind of settlement is largely prohibited today by land use laws.

The Wye system has always been a summer home to great blue herons and ospreys, and winter home to Canada geese and other waterfowl. There is an eagles' nest up the Wye, so it is worthwhile to keep an eye out for one of them. Recreational crabbing is practiced here as a high art, and there are some fat white perch around the docks, fallen trees, and duck blinds.

Canoes, kayaks, rowboats, and small powerboats are all appropriate for the Wye. In a self-propelled boat, explore the coves and creeks of Wye Island that front on the Narrows or the Wye East. Granary Creek and Dividing Creek on the south side of the island are especially nice, though they are two to three miles from Wye and Skipton landings. In an outboard skiff, the whole system becomes available.

The usual caveats apply. Be careful of wakes from large powerboats, mind the rules of the road in what can be at least moderate cruising boat traffic on weekends in the lower river. At all times respect private property. Beyond those, the Wye is the most pastoral of the Bay's rivers, well worth spending some time with.

In the rest of the Eastern Bay/Wye River/Miles River complex, there are lots of short side creeks and coves to explore, and plenty of public landings in Queen Anne's County and Talbot County to put boats overboard, but these waterways are generally more built up than the Wye and don't lend themselves as readily to canoes and kayaks. With an outboard skiff, however, exploration of the Miles River can make for an interesting day. Talbot County's Oak Creek Landing on Rt. 33 going into St. Michaels (call 410-822-2955) would make a good launch point.

The Choptank is a great river system for small boats, especially the upper portion. The Chesapeake Bay Foundation's Maryland Canoe Fleet works regularly on Kings Creek (about five miles east of Easton), Hunting Creek (about two miles southwest of Preston), and Tuckahoe Creek (about eight miles east of Rt. 50 parallel to a line between Wye Mills and Easton). There are several other interesting areas as well. Since Kings Creek is described in detail below, we'll skip it for now and begin with a general discussion of the other parts of the river.

The Choptank is navigable even above Denton to Greensboro. Both are old towns that served as upriver ports in colonial times. The river was settled on both sides by tobacco planters as early as the midseventeenth century, with landings on the outsides of many of the curves and with many ferries. Freight and passengers traveled by schooner and steamboat on the river until about 1930, so many of the landings that show on the maps were lively places in those days. Tuckahoe Creek, a small river in its own right, is navigable up to Wayman's Wharf, once the port for the town of Hillsboro, so it too saw plenty of traffic.

From Greensboro down to Choptank Wharf (the port for Preston, at the mouth of Hunting Creek), the river winds back and forth in big, looping meanders with marshes on the insides and high ground on the outsides of the turns. The Tuckahoe follows the same pattern. In the section from Greensboro to Ganeys Wharf, just below the Tuckahoe's mouth, the river is normally fresh, and the character of the marshes reflects that fact in large stands of arrow arum, pickerelweed, and wild rice. As the water becomes brackish, the marshes turn to huge stands of big cordgrass, but if you follow any of the side creeks, including the short guts that drain the marshes themselves, you'll find plenty of freshwater plants in the upper portions.

The river is powerful here, with strong tides and downstream currents. A measure of its power is the depths of the water in the outsides of the curves. The hole in the turn at Kingston Landing (just above Kings Creek) is fifty-four feet deep, with strong tide rips.

This heavy water movement is the environment in which the Choptank's rockfish have developed their eggs over the past ten thousand or so years. During spring spawning (April and May), the river from

Dover Bridge, just below Kingston Landing, upstream to Two Johns is full of rock of all sizes. For several centuries, watermen ran haul seines and drift nets through the straight reaches in this section of the river, catching thousands of tons. Today that fishing is prohibited, but state fisheries biologists watch the spawning season closely, surveying and analyzing the spawning stock, egg production, and water quality conditions. You'll see them at work if you're on the river in the spring.

You'll also see eagles and, in season, ospreys and waterfowl. The land along the river is farmed intensively, but there are enough marshes and woodlands to give these birds good habitat, at least at present. All three counties along the river (Caroline, Talbot, and Dorchester) are growing in population, so habitat protection and preservation of open space are concerns.

The Tuckahoe too has extensive marshes and woodlands. In fact, some of its shoreline is protected from development by hardwood swamps of maple, black gum, and ash that add to the habitat and food provided by the creek's extensive tidal fresh marshes.

Good landings are plentiful. Ramps for all kinds of small boats are available at Greensboro (410-479-3721), Denton (410-479-1418), Martinak State Park (410-479-1619), Ganeys Wharf (410-479-3721), and Choptank Wharf (410-479-3721) on the Choptank, and Tuckahoe Landing (410-770-8052) near the mouth of the creek. Additional landings for canoes, kayaks, and small aluminum skiffs include Two Johns (410-479-3721) and Kingston Landing (410-770-8052) on the Choptank, and Coveys Landing (410-770-8052) and Hillsboro (410-479-3721) on the Tuckahoe. There is a sandy beach at the mouth of Hunting Creek that is adequate for small boats. CBF has used it often for canoes.

Hunting Creek, by the way, is well worth exploring. It does not have the beautiful high wooded banks of Kings Creek, but it grows a lot of fish, including white perch, channel catfish, largemouth bass, and carp. A good friend fishes it all winter and always finds something to eat, especially perch and cats.

Below Choptank Wharf, the Choptank River widens out, so the best areas to explore are side creeks, most of them brackish. There are plenty more landings all the way down to Cambridge and out past Oxford to Tilghman Island, but most of this water is better for cruising boats than for canoes, kayaks, and skiffs. The Tred Avon's various brackish arms above Oxford are good for outboards, but even they are a bit wide for canoes and kayaks. Make no mistake—these are pretty waterways, but the best small boat water lies upstream.

Below the Choptank lie the Little Choptank River and Slaughter Creek, which flows down through the marshes behind Taylors Island to the head of the Honga River. Their marshes are brackish. There are commercial ramps available on the Little Choptank and at the mouth of Slaughter Creek. The latter area is interesting to explore in a big skiff, but it is a bit wide for good canoe/kayak exploration. If you go into the Slaughter Creek marsh ("The Broads"), take a NOAA chart and be *very* careful. This is a tricky area. If you run aground on a falling tide, you may find that the bottom is too thick to move the boat but too thin to walk on. It is not a nice place to spend the night.

Trip Description: Kings Creek

With so much good water, it is difficult to pick out one area to describe in detail, but Kings Creek gets the nod because of its high, wooded banks upstream and its extensive marshes. It has both beauty and variety.

Type of Waterway—Tidal fresh/brackish creek

Directions and Access—To reach Kings Creek, take Rt. 331, Dover Road, east from Rt. 50 in Easton. Two and one-half miles down the road, make a 45-degree left turn onto Kingston Road (the 90-degree left is Black Dog Alley). The first creek that Kingston Road crosses is Kings Creek. You can launch a canoe or a kayak at the bridge or on the main stem of the Choptank at Kingston Landing. To reach Kingston Landing, continue over the bridge, turn right when the road comes to a T, and follow to the river (about one mile total from the bridge).

For cartop outboard skiffs, put over at Kingston Landing. For skiffs on trailers, put over either at Tuckahoe Landing, just inside the mouth of Tuckahoe Creek (410-770-8052), or Ganeys Wharf on the main river (410-479-3721), and run down to the creek mouth.

Trip Routes—Kings Creek is long enough that it is quite possible to spend a whole day poking around either the section above the bridge or the section below, each of which has its own character. The best sampler for a canoe or kayak trip is to put overboard at the Kingston Road bridge and explore both upstream and down. Choose your route according to the tide.

If you decide to concentrate on the upstream portion, simply paddle up from the bridge and back down. If you want to explore the lower portion, check the tide. Then begin at either the bridge or Kingston Landing and paddle with it. When you get to your takeout, you can walk back to get your car in twenty minutes.

Cautions—Beware of the strong Choptank tides; do not swim at Kingston Landing (remember the depth and the tide rips). If the wind is more than ten knots, put over at the bridge and stay well up in the creek.

Comments—Finding Kings Creek is always a surprise. The landscape through which it flows is typically Eastern Shore: wide open soybean and corn fields interspersed with a few white and yellow farmhouses surrounded by trees. It looks a lot like the Midwest. The creek itself is hardly the center of this landscape. Rather it is a stream hidden and protected by a thin blanket of trees. As you drive along Kingston Road toward the put-in spots, you will get only an occasional glimpse of it. Likewise, when you paddle along, you hardly catch sight of the landscape you drove across; the view is obstructed by tree-lined banks along the upper stretches and broad expanses of marsh below. This seemingly untouched quality and the variety of habitats in a three-mile stretch make Kings Creek a jewel for small boats.

It is worth exploring at all times of year: in the summer the floodplain trees along the upper creek banks provide shade from the sun, and in the winter the same trees provide shelter from strong northwest winds. Likewise, when a summer breeze is sorely needed to wipe away the season's customary outbreak of mosquitoes, the lower reaches of the creek provide open water and open marshland across which that breeze can blow unimpeded.

If you look on a detailed Talbot County map, you will find that the creek begins at an old millpond. This pond is typical of many of the smaller Eastern Shore tributaries. After periods of heavy rainfall (notably the spring), canoes can make the voyage around and under downed logs to reach the pond. If you do make it to the pond, you can barely see the raised bank defining its dam because it is so overgrown. The trees on the bank are at least ninety years old, marking its construction at some time prior to that date.

These upper regions—above the marsh line—are rarely explored. They provide excellent habitat in which to find wildlife: green herons, wood ducks, and, during the migrations, warblers. One of the most memorable times we have had on Kings Creek was canoeing at night in the upper creek area. It was a warm summer evening and in fact the only time of day cool enough to venture outside. The tide was very high because the moon was full, and the moonlight illuminated our path.

The creek was alive. Nature guides and handbooks always talk about nocturnal animals, and occasionally we see them during the day, but that night no explaining was necessary. A great horned owl continually let out its call, a screech owl was close by, and two otters were swimming along the marsh edge, perhaps fishing for menhaden that had come into the creek to filter plankton. The scene illustrated the extraordinary diversity of life in the Bay's tidal creeks.

As the hawk flies, it is one mile from the creek's upper reaches to the bridge, but because the creek flows around many tight meanders, the distance by water is three miles. The outsides of the meanders are high banks of mature hardwoods, especially beeches and oaks. The marshes on the insides are tidal fresh, with wooded swamp trees like black gum, ash, and red maple mixed in.

Around the bridge, you may notice the first signs of salt water if you are sharp-eyed. Some of the fallen trees will have barnacles growing on them. These are low-salinity species, but they don't grow in completely fresh water.

From here on down, start looking for changes. The wooded banks will continue for a quarter-mile or so, but then the creek will open out to flow through broad marshes of brackish water species like big cordgrass, tidemarsh waterhemp, and marsh hibiscus.

The meanders will continue, looping through a dozen turns on the way down to the Choptank. No matter how many times we paddle Kings Creek, there always seems to be one more curve than we expected to get to the river.

Just before the creek reaches the river, there is a good place to explore the marshes without getting your feet wet. The Maryland Chapter of The Nature Conservancy has built and maintains a half-mile-long boardwalk at the mouth of the creek. From it the viewer can observe migratory and resident birdlife, muskrat lodges (especially visible in the winter), and a variety of freshwater marsh plants. The marsh plants are easy to pick out because they are illustrated and labeled on corresponding plaques.

Despite Kings Creek's beauty, fish are not its strong point. Nonetheless, we have, over the years, caught pickerel, bass, bluegills, channel catfish, white catfish, shiners, menhaden, white perch, yellow perch, and carp. Like all the creeks, abundance of fish varies with the seasons. Kings does have fair-sized yellow and white perch runs, but not as memorable as those in other creeks or in the main river. Carp are easy to spot during their spring spawning because they stir up large clouds of silt when boats approach them. The largest fish we've caught in Kings Creek was a twenty-pound carp so full of eggs that touching her caused some to spew out.

We often see river otters on the upper stretches of the creek. Laying eyes on otters can be difficult because they are very secretive. A loud, careless group can doubtless pass the otter without recognizing its presence. Likewise, a party in a hurry, unwilling to explore the marsh edges and downed trees for signs, will certainly leave the area without knowing when the otter was there.

The last part of the trip leads the boater to Kingston Landing. This is an old steamboat wharf, and a prime illustration of how such wharves were sited in the nineteenth century, when the river was still a highway. As noted above, the channel swings in close to the bank, providing fastland for construction of the wharf and plenty of deep water (fifty feet just fifteen feet from shore). You'll see the tide rips on the surface as the current boils through the turn, and if you search with a depth-sounder, you will find the fifty-four-foot hole just downriver of the wharf.

Although there aren't any steamers moving up the Choptank, Kingston Landing is an enjoyable spot to relax prior to the drive home. Ospreys nest on the channel marker across the river, local folks fish for catfish and white perch, and the Choptank is always moving past.

Blackwater, Transquaking, and Nanticoke Rivers

The lower part of Dorchester County, south of Cambridge and southwest of Rt. 50, is a vast complex of swamp and marsh. The land is very flat, with elevations of less than fifteen feet. Streams have their origins in deep wooded swamps and flow in countless meanders through wide open marsh. It is big sky country. Dorchester is the second-largest county in Maryland, and it has more wetlands than any other county in Maryland or Virginia. Much of this marsh country is drained by two river systems, the Blackwater and the Transquaking. There are four good access points and plenty for the small boat explorer to see and do.

It would take a long time to explore this area completely by small boat. A good starting point is to visit the Blackwater National Wildlife Refuge, drive the wildlife drive, climb the observation tower, and look at the exhibits in the visitor center (410-228-2677 for information). While there, ask about boat access to the Blackwater and Little Blackwater rivers. The waterways within the refuge are generally closed from

December through April to keep people away from bald eagle nests. There is, however, good fishing from the bank at the bridge over the Little Blackwater, just east of the refuge office on Key Wallace Drive, and on Rt. 335, just west of the visitor center where the road crosses the Blackwater.

The best boat access to the Blackwater is at Shorters Wharf, just south of the refuge on Maple Dam Road. Call Dorchester County (410-228-2920) for information. The Shorters Wharf ramp is sometimes covered with silt. It can be tricky to get anything larger than a sixteen-foot johnboat overboard here.

Be very careful if you put overboard at Shorters Wharf and go back up into the refuge. Take a map and a compass. The channel can be difficult to follow, as it simply snakes through open water in some areas, and the flats around it are very shallow. If you fetch up on one of them, you will find that it is too thick to pole through but too soft to walk on. Tides are irregular, driven more by wind than by moon, so there is no regular cycle of high and low water. Like Slaughter Creek, this is not a nice place to spend the night.

The Transquaking system lies east of the Blackwater, hidden in wooded swamps between that river system and Rt. 50. Most people headed south on the highway do not know that it is there. This river has two arms, the one that goes by its own name and the other, the Chicamacomico, to the east. There are good launch ramps for small boats at Higgins Millpond Road on the Transquaking (410-228-2920) and at New Bridge on New Bridge Road on the Chicamacomico (410-228-2920). The run from the Higgins Millpond ramp to the New Bridge ramp is a good one for small outboard skiffs, covering about thirty-five miles. The Chicamacomico is a particularly good fishing area for largemouth bass and crappie within the span from a mile below New Bridge to a mile above. A canoe would be an excellent craft for this kind of fishing.

The only major industry on the Chicamacomico today is Cecil Robbins's Boat Yard at Drawbridge, about three miles below New Bridge. Robbins has long been a builder of top-quality workboats and charter boats. Originally, he worked in cedar and mahogany, but today he molds his hulls in fiberglass and then finishes them out with superb wooden cabinetwork in the cockpits and deckhouses.

There is one good launch ramp on the lower part of the Transquaking, below its junction with the Chicamacomico. This is at Bestpitch Ferry (410-228-2920) on Bestpitch Ferry Road south and east of the Blackwater refuge. It provides easy access to run down the lower part of the Transquaking to the head of Fishing Bay.

This part of the Bay country has always been full of life. As a result, Indians and Europeans alike have lived in it as trappers, fishermen, and hunters for centuries. Even today, the people who live here largely follow these ways of life. In the 1930s, the federal government recognized the value of the Dorchester marshes and set up the Blackwater National Wildlife Refuge, which has preserved an important part of those marshes, provided some new jobs for local people, and built a useful tourist resource for Dorchester County. In the lower parts of the marshes, crabbing, oystering, and boatbuilding are also important.

The Nanticoke River is the eastern margin of Dorchester County. It is a big river fed by a large watershed that begins in Delaware. As it flows through Maryland, it drains parts of Dorchester, Caroline, and Wicomico counties. The Nanticoke is navigable to Seaford, Delaware, and still forms an important transportation artery for hauling petroleum products to the Delmarva Power and Light plant in Vienna and the Du Pont nylon plant in Seaford. The river has two major tributaries, Marshyhope Creek, with Federalsburg at its head of navigation, and Broad Creek, with Laurel, Delaware, at its head. The Marshyhope is described in detail below.

The Nanticoke has always been important as a wide, navigable river that reaches deep into the inland portions of the Shore. The sandy soils around it are not as good for growing grain as those of the upper Shore, but the river was settled early by tobacco planters. It did not attract and hold the kind of gentry that developed in Talbot, Queen Anne's, and Kent counties. In fact, its most storied citizen was a real villain, Patty Cannon—thief, murderer, and slave dealer. She ran a ferry and a tavern on the river near the Maryland/Delaware line as fronts for her other enterprises during the first quarter of the nineteenth century, before she was brought to justice.

A more legitimate business for which the river became justly famous in the second half of the nineteenth century was shipbuilding. There was abundant timber, including good stands of cypress on Broad Creek. Towns like Vienna, Sharptown, and Bethel, Delaware, all located on the outsides of curves, developed into shipbuilding centers. Bethel is known "the home of the rams," the three-masted lumber schooners designed to ply the Bay and to fit through the Chesapeake and Albemarle and Chesapeake and Delaware canals. These large vessels were built between 1880 and 1930 and launched sideways into Broad Creek, which is misnamed: There is plenty of depth but not much width. One of the rams, the *Edwin and Maude*, lived a productive second life from the mid-1950s to the mid-1980s as *Victory Chimes*, a popular cruise schooner on the coast of Maine. Very few people ever suspected that this proud, dark-green-hulled beauty was launched in fresh water 'way up a tributary on the Chesapeake. She survives today on the Great Lakes as *Domino Effect*. *This Was Chesapeake Bay*, by Robert H. Burgess, has a good section on Bethel and its rams.

Historically, the Nanticoke was a major spawning river for rockfish and shad. The area from the mouth of the Marshyhope up to the mouth of Broad Creek has been a traditional rockfish spawning area, and the area around Vienna an important nursery. The drift gill net fishery on this river gave rise in the early twentieth century to a graceful indigenous skiff, the shad barge. These boats were traditionally built in lengths of from eighteen to twenty-two feet, with sweeping sheers and flared sides like New England dories. In the old days, each side of a shad barge was built of a single wide cypress plank. The first ones were designed for oar power, but soon enough they were modified to accept outboards. With the demise of the shad runs and the closure of the rockfish fishery, the building of shad barges has almost died out, but there are a few still on the river being used for recreational purposes.

The extensive wetlands offered by the Dorchester marshes and the Nanticoke make great wildlife habitat. Traditionally, the whole area has held strong waterfowl populations. Blackwater and the Elliott Island Marsh between the head of Fishing Bay and the mouth of the Nanticoke have been particularly important to them. The scattered human population and the isolated stands of loblolly pines out on the marsh have made for excellent eagle habitat as these birds have increased in number during the 1970s and 1980s. Dorchester County is now a major nesting area.

The marshes grow millions of muskrats, upon which has been based a major trapping industry. River otters also abound, as do nutria, a large South American rodent that was introduced to the area in the early part of the century. Nutria, unfortunately, cause serious problems. They tear up and eat out the rootstocks of the marsh plants, causing marshes to deteriorate and break up into open water. There is a disturbing trend of loss of wetlands in the Dorchester marshes over the last thirty years, due apparently to a combination of sea level rise and an overabundance of nutria.

The area also serves fishermen well, especially those who delight in variety. The fresh water at the upper ends of the Blackwater and Transquaking systems and of the Nanticoke offer largemouth bass, crappie, chain pickerel, yellow perch, and the ubiquitous white perch. Farther down, there are more white perch, plus rockfish, and in the lower rivers, trout and spot. There is a strong crab industry at the head of Fishing Bay and at the mouth of the Nanticoke. Both areas have historically been important oyster-growing areas, though they have suffered in recent years, as have virtually all the Bay's oyster grounds.

The Nanticoke has good access. There is a boat ramp at Seaford, favored especially in the winter by fishermen looking for yellow perch and chain pickerel around the hot-water discharge pipe at the power plant there. There is a good ramp at Cherry Beach Park in Sharptown (410-883-3767), plus others at Vienna (410-228-2920), Mardela Springs (at the head of Barren Creek: 410-548-4900), and Wetipquin (on the lower river: 410-548-4900). There are also landings on the Marshyhope, but more of that below.

The river above Vienna is largely tidal fresh, and the ramps at Vienna and Sharptown provide excellent access to it. A good place to explore in an outboard skiff is Chicone Creek, just above Vienna on the Dorchester side. For canoes, kayaks, and rowing vessels, Barren Creek is a beautiful, winding waterway easily reached from the ramp at Mardela Springs. If you have two cars, it makes a good trip to paddle from Vienna to Mardela Springs, or vice versa, depending on the tide. Be careful in self-propelled boats in the open river, however, since tides are very strong and you will occasionally find tugs with barges in the channel. Farther downriver, the boat ramp over Wetipquin Creek on Wetipquin Road just northeast of Tyaskin is a good access point. Wetipquin Creek is brackish, and a good area to explore by canoe or kayak. It is also possible in good weather to paddle across the river and explore the shores of Elliott Island. Outboard skiffs are also appropriate for this area, especially for running upriver to explore Quantico and Rewastico creeks on the Wicomico side a couple of miles north.

Trip Description: Marshyhope Creek

Type of Waterway—Tidal fresh

Directions and Access—Federalsburg Marina Park (410-754-8173) or the VFW ramp on Rosser Road just south of Federalsburg. Also Brookview Public Landing just off Rt. 14 by the bridge between Brookview and Eldorado.

Trip Routes—In a powerboat, the best move is to put overboard at Federalsburg, run downriver and run back. In a canoe or kayak, paddle down from Federalsburg to Brookview or back up, depending on the tide. The landing at Brookview is marginal at best, suitable only for self-propelled vessels or cartop outboard skiffs. It is also possible to paddle all the way down to Sharptown, but that makes for a trip of fully ten miles, which does not allow much time for poking around.

Cautions—The banks of the Marshyhope include extensive wooded swamps, so there are not many places to get out of the river in the event of bad weather. If you are on it in the summertime, be particularly careful of thunderstorms. If you are in a self-propelled boat, build your trip around the tide as much as you can, since the currents are powerful. On weekends, there is a good deal of traffic from bass fishermen in high-powered outboard boats. Most of these people are knowledgeable and courteous, but there are a few throttle jockeys among them, so it pays to be careful. If you are running a powerboat in the spring before the lily pads come up, be careful to follow the channel. At high tide, it will not be obvious. Also, if you are in a large powerboat, be careful of the vertical clearance under the Harrison Ferry bridge between Federalsburg and Brookview. It is only about six feet above high tide.

Comments—The Marshyhope is a beautiful, deep, winding river that runs between wooded swamp of ash, black gum, and red maple on the one hand and high wooded banks on the other. The upper section between Federalsburg and Harrison Ferry includes a number of old gravel pits which have been abandoned long enough that they have grown some marsh plants and shrubbery around their margins. These are excellent areas for crappie and bass. You will notice a few old landings (on the outsides of turns, naturally), including Browns Landing, an old farm wharf just above Harrison Ferry. There is a deep hole just off Browns Landing that is well worth fishing for bass and catfish. You will also notice in this part of the river that there are extensive marshes and backwater creeks. These too are well worth exploration.

In a dry summer, you may also notice irrigation pumps drawing water from the creek to irrigate land along it. This part of Dorchester County is an important produce-growing area. The towns just to the west, Williamsburg, East New Market, and Hurlock, are all railroad settlements that grew up around the shipping of farm products. Today, of course, most of that produce is shipped by truck and railroad, but at the turn of the century, it was shipped by steamboat. When you get to

Brookview, you will find a reminder of this era, a large drawbridge that was designed for a navigable river. The Marshyhope is no longer buoyed by the U.S. Coast Guard, and the Harrison Ferry bridge is fixed at low clearance, as you will have already noticed, so the age of commercial traffic on the creek is long past. The only vestige of it is the Brookview bridge, which was built in the early part of this century.

Today, there is very little population growth along the Marshyhope, which helps add to its charms. It is one of the Bay country's real jewels.

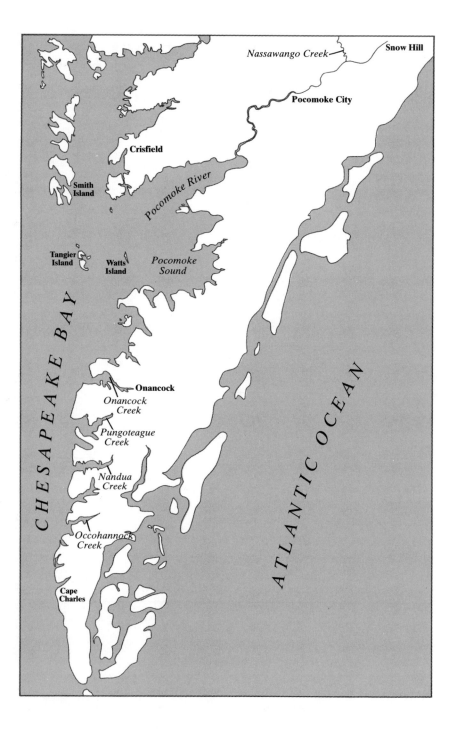

seven

Lower Eastern Shore

Wicomico, Manokin, and
Pocomoke Rivers, Virginia Bayside Creeks

The Wicomico River is always a surprise. It is a substantial waterway that has allowed the city of Salisbury to grow over the past 250 years. The city is at the head of navigation, with enough high land around it to provide waterpower for mills during the nineteenth century. What is left from that era is a collection of small, pretty lakes like Johnson Pond. Call the city (410-548-4900) for information. The ponds are canoeable, and they have good fishing.

The river in the city is narrow and deep, with a surprising amount of life for an industrialized waterway. Good access for canoes, kayaks, rowing skiffs, and outboards is provided by the Riverside Boat Ramp, on Riverside Drive just south of Rt. 50. This is a public facility, with plenty of parking. Call 410-548-4900 for information. If you put overboard here, be careful of tug and barge traffic and of powerboats.

This part of the river is tidal fresh, and the industrial section gives way about a mile below the ramp to a series of wild rice marshes, with residential areas interspersed. Fishing is good, especially downtide of pilings, docks, and fallen trees. The river has bass, crappie, catfish, and white perch.

There are two working ferries down the river, at Upper Ferry and Whitehaven. Be careful when passing them, but by all means watch them, and if you have occasion to use them, do so. In addition to a pleasant short ride, they can make auto travel to and from the area below Salisbury much easier. The river is fresh to Upper Ferry, but it begins to get brackish below there.

There are two access points on the lower river. The Redden Ferry ramp is on Wicomico Creek, a large tidal creek appropriate for both outboard skiffs and paddle/oar craft. The road into Redden Ferry is rough, but the ramp will serve outboard boats up to twenty feet or so. Call Wicomico County (410-548-4900) for information. Near the mouth of the river is the town of Mount Vernon, a sleepy area that once bustled with a shipyard and several other industrial installations. Webster's Cove Harbor (410-651-0749) provides a boat ramp. This water is most suitable for larger outboard skiffs. If you put overboard here, you can run upriver, but it is also worthwhile to go down to the mouth of the Wicomico and turn south into Monie Bay, Monie Creek, and Little Monie Creek. The Monie creeks are all but forgotten corners of the Bay country, and they are pretty waterways.

The Manokin is a short but pleasant river with a good transition from tidal fresh to brackish water. Like other rivers in the area, it was settled early and farmed. The town of Princess Anne grew up in 1731 at the head of navigation. It has been the county seat for many years, and it is on the railroad line that runs down the Eastern Shore. These factors made it prosperous in the nineteenth and early twentieth centuries. The river has silted in now, but in those days, schooners called at wharves that are now covered by the marshes you see as you go by on Rt. 50. The town is developing a park, quite possibly with a launch point for canoes and cartop skiffs (call 410-651-1818 for information). Other local access points include Raccoon Point at the river's mouth for small boats and the St. Peter's Creek ramp for larger skiffs (410-651-1930 for both). The Manokin is overlooked, but it is a pretty river with nice marshes. It also has a major tributary to explore, Kings Creek.

Below the Manokin, the Big and Little Annemessex rivers are interesting, but they are suitable only for big outboard skiffs. The inside channel behind Janes Island, the mouth of the Little Annessex, Broad Creek, and the Cedar Island Marsh below Crisfield are all interesting, but there is a lot of workboat traffic, and the broad open waters argue against any vessel less than sixteen feet in length in even the calmest weather. Any kind of a blow will require an even larger boat. It is important to be careful in exploring these marshes. Like the Slaughter Creek Broads and Blackwater, this is an easy place to get stuck and a bad place to spend the night. Call Somers Cove Marina in Crisfield (410-

968-0925) and Janes Island State Park (410-968-1565) for information on launch ramps and other facilities.

Below Crisfield, the Pocomoke River flows into Pocomoke Sound. This is a beautiful long river, rising in the southwest corner of Delaware. It holds the northernmost bald cypress swamp of any size on the Atlantic Coast. The land was farmed in the seventeenth century for tobacco, but settlement along it was sparse. There is relatively little fastland close to the river. The town of Snow Hill was founded at the head of navigation in the late seventeenth century.

Pocomoke City, below Snow Hill, has had a ferry since that time, but the town that grew up around it has had several names. It was not christened Pocomoke City until 1878. Local lumber and good access to deep water made it a shipbuilding center early in its history. The Industrial Revolution, with its increased demand for timber, caused the development of sawmills in the 1840s, and lumber became an important trade item. Steamboats provided the primary connection with the outside world during the period 1870 to 1930. Schooners continued to carry lumber out into the 1930s, and powerboats were used for some years after that. The last of the sailing freighters on the Bay came up past Pocomoke City to Snow Hill for fertilizer until the early 1950s. They included the schooner *Mattie F. Dean* and the ram *Edward R. Baird*. Tug and barge traffic continues on the river today, serving a plywood plant just below Pocomoke City.

The area between Snow Hill and Pocomoke also produced bog iron in the eighteenth and nineteenth centuries, especially at the head of Nassawango Creek, of which there will be more description below. Bog iron is produced by bacteria. It is a crude ore with no commercial value today, but it served an important purpose in this area 150 to 200 years ago.

On the river below Pocomoke City, the small towns of Rehobeth and Shelltown grew up around landings on the outsides of curves. Rehobeth is known primarily for its Presbyterian church, which was founded in 1705 by the famous preacher Francis Makemie.

The Pocomoke was important for its commercial fisheries years ago, and there is still one family running a large operation out of Shelltown, but otherwise the fisheries have declined. The river, however, is still valuable for its sportfisheries, especially largemouth bass and crappie.

Much of the timber along the south side of the river between Snow Hill and Pocomoke City is now incorporated into the Pocomoke State

Forest. The virgin timber has been cut over, but there is good mature second growth. The forest along the river is beautiful for much of the spring, summer, and fall, from the early green growth of the cypress in April to the rich fall colors in October. Spring brings one especially beautiful migratory bird, the apricot- and olive-colored prothonotary warbler.

Access to the river above Snow Hill for canoes includes the bridges at Whiton's Crossing and Porter's Crossing. The run down from Whiton's is tricky and should not be attempted without someone who has already travelled the route. The run from Porter's Crossing is a pleasant four-mile paddle and an excellent introduction to the upper river. Lower access points for canoes, kayaks, rowboats, and outboards include Shad Landing and Milburn Landing in the Pocomoke River State Park (410-632-2566), Byrd Park in Snow Hill, Winter Quarters Park and Cypress Park in Pocomoke City, Rehobeth, and Shelltown (410-632-3766).

The swamp comes right down to the river with only small pockets of marsh along the main stem all the way from Whiton's and Porter's crossings down past Snow Hill and Pocomoke City nearly to Rehobeth. From there, large brackish marshes continue to the river's mouth. From Pocomoke City down, the river winds in looping meanders, and the channel is very deep. It is always interesting to watch a tug and barge negotiate the bends. If you put overboard at Rehobeth, a nice creek runs deep into the marsh opposite the ramp. If you run down to the river mouth below Shelltown, be careful of the shoals on either side of the dredged channel that runs out into Pocomoke Sound.

Opposite Shelltown is Pitts Creek, in Virginia, with a boat landing of its own (804-787-3900). Pitts is a beautiful, long, winding creek that comes down from a millpond. It has good fishing, even in winter, for rockfish and perch. In summertime, the upper section, which is tidal fresh, has a great collection of marsh flowers.

Below the Pocomoke, the creeks of Virginia's Eastern Shore are short but beautiful. All are brackish. These include Onancock Creek, Pungoteague Creek, Nandua Creek, and Occohannock Creek. Each of these has a landing on it: Onancock Landing on Onancock Creek (804-367-1000), Harborton Landing on Pungoteague Creek (804-787-3900), Hacks Neck Landing at the mouth of Nandua Creek (804-787-3900), and Morely's Wharf on Occohannock Creek (804-367-1000). Cape Charles Harbor has a ramp too (804-367-1000), but this is broad open water, not small boat territory. Fishing is excellent, but don't think about it unless your boat is at least eighteen feet long.

There are some wonderful areas to explore on the seaside of Virginia's Eastern Shore as well, but that's another story. The channels in behind the barrier islands are hard to spot, and the tides are very strong. If you venture over there, be careful and seek advice in a fishing center like Wachapreague or Oyster.

Trip Description: Nassawango Creek, Pocomoke River

Type of Waterway—Tidal fresh

Directions and Access—For canoes, put overboard at the road crossing at Red House Road, off Rt. 12 between Salisbury and Snow Hill. Paddle down about four miles and take out at the road crossing for River Road. If you are in a kayak or a rowboat, you can try to come down from Red House Road, but the creek is very narrow, and you may find that, for the first mile, a double-bladed paddle or pair of oars is a hindrance. If you are in an outboard skiff, put overboard at Shad Landing Area of Pocomoke River State Park or Byrd Park in Snow Hill and travel up, but be careful of submerged logs and cypress knees.

Cautions—Nassawango Creek is a well-protected waterway and so is relatively safe in almost any weather. Be aware, however, that the surrounding trees will block your view of the sky, so that you will not be able to see approaching thunderstorms, which can be very dangerous. Plan your trips in the summertime so that you are off the water by early afternoon to minimize the risk of storms. There are very few takeouts on the creek between Red House Road and River Road. In fall or spring when the water is cold, an overturned boat can be a real problem. Be prepared ahead of time.

Comments—Nassawango Creek is classic flat water. It winds back and forth, cutting its way through small islands of cypress in its lower reaches. If you are in doubt about which way to go, follow the flow downstream. The banks are almost entirely swamp, although there is one pretty little rice marsh about a half-mile below Red House Road. The creek is very deep, even close to the bank. If you have a sonar, you will find that even though it is only thirty feet across just below Red House Road, it is ten to twelve feet deep in spots. About a mile below Red House Road, the creek begins to widen out. Be sure to explore its islands and backwaters. The Nature Conservancy deserves a great deal of credit for preserving several tracts of swamp and creek bank.

Look at the cypress trees in detail. They are true wetland plants, growing with their roots completely submerged. There is speculation that they use their knees, which protrude above water, to get oxygen down to their roots, but research on the subject is inconclusive. In any case, the complex of roots and knees around each tree provides excellent habitat, especially for fish like largemouth bass, crappie, white perch, and yellow perch.

Cypress is also unusual in that it is a deciduous conifer, one of only two native to North America (the other is larch). In spring, its newly emerging needles are a beautiful soft green. In fall, before they drop, they turn a russet heather mixture of tones against the brilliant colors of the surrounding gums, maples, and ashes.

The Pocomoke does not have a monopoly on cypress in the Chesapeake. Virginia has several excellent swamps. Still, this river is well endowed, and Nassawango is as good a place to study a cypress swamp as any. Take your time exploring it. It is wonderful.

eight

Upper Western Shore

Susquehanna, Bush, Gunpowder, Middle, Back, Patapsco, Magothy, Severn, South, Rhode, and West Rivers

The upper western shore rivers are mostly short and heavily settled. The shortness results from their being squeezed between the Susquehanna watershed to the north and the Patuxent to the south and west. The headwaters of these rivers drain largely from the middle of the populous Baltimore/Washington corridor, and all of this land is within fifty miles of the Baltimore or Washington metropolitan areas. The land in this section of the Bay country rolls and folds, with lots of coves and creeks, and thus a long shoreline. Three hundred years ago, the area attracted tobacco farmers, and, in fact, a few of their descendants are growing that crop today. Now, however, the upper western shore mostly attracts commuters who want to live on the water, so over the past thirty years, much of the shoreline has been developed. The waterways are broad and deep, so the area is beloved of cruising yachtsmen and well described in the standard cruise guides.

In spite of the houses and the traffic, if you choose carefully, there are some pleasant and interesting places to explore in small boats. Do some homework ahead of time, using the ideas here and anything you can glean from the cruise guides. Study the charts, looking for creeks and coves that appear to have few houses. There is a special kind of satisfaction in finding natural jewels hidden among large numbers of people.

The Susquehanna itself is tidal for about eight miles from its head of navigation at Smith Falls, just below Conowingo Dam. Remember,

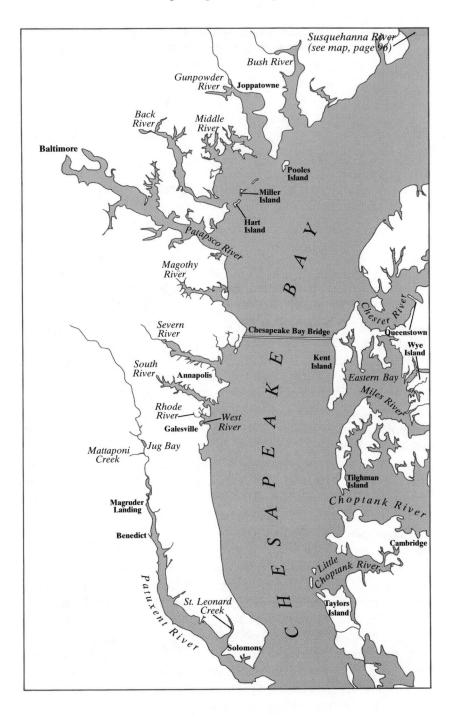

though, how powerful this river is. It is a mile wide, and in one place it is over eighty feet deep. Even though this section is tidal, a major storm is capable of making the water rise over twenty feet. You will see smaller boats on it, but sixteen- to eighteen- foot skiffs provide a good margin of safety.

Be *very* careful above Port Deposit, where there are many rocks both submerged and exposed, and especially powerful currents. Release of water from Conowingo Dam can cause special problems, especially for anchored boats. The fishing is good, but it is wise to go with a guide the first time. Contact local tackle shops for names and addresses. There are several good access points. Call Susquehanna State Park (410-557-7994) and Harford County (410-638-3570) for information on launch ramps, especially Tydings Memorial Park and Roberts Park in the city.

While in Havre de Grace, check the Decoy Museum and the Susquehanna and Tidewater Canal Lock House Museum. The former has wonderful exhibits of the glory days of waterfowling on the Susquehanna Flats, and the latter gives a glimpse into the era when freight was transported down from central Pennsylvania by canal to be loaded onto sailing ships in Havre de Grace.

Once you get onto the river, you will find a number of things to look at, especially the big Arundel Corporation stone quarry just upriver. This operation is unusual because it is a large and productive stone quarry juxtaposed with a deep-water landing. Arundel Corporation is able to operate much larger barges out of this quarry than most of the other materials companies on other Bay rivers. The economies of scale from the large barges give them a competitive advantage in a number of markets. By all means watch the quarrying operations from the river, but be very careful not to get in the way of either the barges or their towboats.

Poking around in the river between Havre de Grace and Port Deposit is relatively easy if you remember to be careful about traffic and to watch the wind, which can be quite strong. With the high, rocky banks, it feels like being on one of the Bay's other big western shore rivers above the fall line, say on the James just above the city of Richmond, except that the Susquehanna absolutely dwarfs you. Just remember that while the James may be a powerful river, the Susquehanna is far and away the largest on the Atlantic Coast.

While you are up in this section marveling at the river's size, note the eighty-foot hole on the back side of Garrett Island near Perryville. If you are fishing for bass or catfish, pay attention to the pilings on the various bridges and to the grass beds around Garrett Island. Keep an eye out for eagles and, in season, ospreys.

Just below Garrett Island, the Susquehanna opens out onto the flats, and its currents slow down. Centuries of riverborne sediments have collected here, so that the depth goes from fifty feet to only two feet in a mile. There are two channels around the edge of the flats, but the water is very shallow on either side of them. By all means explore the two small islands out by the Fishing Battery Lighthouse on the flats, but be very careful anywhere in this area of running into shallow water, tangling a propeller in grass, or hitting a log. The river carries a lot of debris down here.

What you will learn if you visit the Decoy Museum is that the flats once formed one of the finest habitats in North America for fish and waterfowl, largely as a result of extensive beds of submerged wild celery and other low-salinity species of submerged grasses. A build-up of nutrient pollution and sediments over the last thirty years has caused these plants serious problems. Hurricane Agnes in 1972 dropped a century's worth of sediments in several days. The wild celery and other Bay grasses have come back only slowly since then, but the flats are still a place to watch. Any improvements in water quality that Pennsylvania makes to the Susquehanna over the next ten years will pay big dividends on the flats.

Below the mouth of the Susquehanna, the shoreline is restricted tightly by the Army's Aberdeen Proving Ground. Restricted areas are marked on the charts and tightly patrolled. Respect those restricted areas and do not, under any circumstances, go ashore. The area is loaded with unexploded ordnance. Ironically, the lack of people on the Aberdeen Proving Ground has made it an excellent roosting spot for bald eagles, one of the four best on the Bay. Do keep your eyes out for the big birds.

The next two rivers down the Bay, the Bush and the Gunpowder, display an interesting geological pattern. Both have relatively long watersheds that stretch back into the piedmont region of Harford County, but as they flow downstream and cross the fall line onto the coastal plain, they open suddenly into broad tidal waters, in both cases just east of Rt. 40. Our ignorance of soil conservation over the past 300 years has produced terrible erosion in the upper watersheds, with sediments flowing swiftly downstream out of the piedmont to collect by the thousands of cubic yards in braided deltas at the heads of navigation on the rivers. The only other portion of the Bay country where this pattern is repeated is on the Virginia side of the Potomac between Mount Vernon and Quantico, where creeks like Accotink, Pohick, Occoquan, and Quantico have all built great deltas over the last two centuries. There will be more on these in a later chapter.

The sediment build-up has caused tremendous loss of deep-water habitat and has closed these areas to any vessels except canoes and outboard skiffs, but it has provided interesting complexes of marsh to explore. On the Bush and Gunpowder rivers, these are good mixed tidal fresh marshes full of yellow perch, bass, crappie, white perch, and waterfowl.

For access to Otter Point Creek at the head of the Bush, use Otter Point Public Landing, Flying Point Park, or Willoughby Beach Landing (410-638-3570 for all three). Otter Point Public Landing is the best for canoes, since it means minimum exposure to windswept, shallow, open waters.

The Gunpowder is a longer, stronger river than the Bush, with lots of history. See the trip description below.

With the exception of the Patapsco, the rest of the rivers in this part of the Bay are short and slow flowing. To understand these waterways, it helps to remember that the upper Chesapeake Bay is really the tidal Susquehanna. The rivers and creeks function partly as tidal inlets. In addition to what comes out of their own watersheds, all receive large quantities of fresh water from the Susquehanna and salty water from the lower Bay on the rising tides. The mixing of brackish lower Bay water, the Susquehanna's fresh water, and local fresh water makes for complex flow patterns. After heavy rains in central Pennsylvania, the Severn, for example, is sometimes fresher at its mouth than in its midsection. The result of this mixing is unusual combinations of tidal fresh and brackish waters.

The first two of these waterways are Middle River and Back River, both squeezed between the Gunpowder and Patapsco watersheds. Both are heavily built up, with lots of traffic. Outboard skiffs are better choices than paddle/oar craft here. Perhaps the best areas are Dundee and Seneca creeks just above Middle River. Use the Hammerman Area of Gunpowder Falls State Park (410-592-2897) for launching. At the mouth of Back River, Hart-Miller Island and Black Marsh are both worth exploring. Use Rocky Point Park (410-887-3616) for launching. Hart-Miller Island is under construction as a diked dredge spoil disposal site, and some of the area is restricted, but the beach area facing into Back River is very pleasant, even if it is crowded on summer weekends.

The Patapsco is a substantial river that rises in the eastern portion of Carroll County. It too has carried a great deal of silt over the years, with the result that its head of navigation has moved downstream from Elkridge to the Hanover Street bridge on Rt. 2. A century ago, the marshes at the bridge, right by what is now Harbor Hospital Center, had excellent stands of tidal fresh vegetation and all the wildlife that it supports.

Over the years, silt, industrial development, and sewage have degraded the lower Patapsco, but Clean Water Act improvements to industrial discharges and sewage are causing improvements now. Wide water and heavy shipping traffic dictate larger skiffs (sixteen feet or longer) and *great* care around commercial vessels, but the area is interesting to explore. Read Bob Keith's *Baltimore Harbor* for background. Look for waterfowl in Middle Branch just below the Hanover Street bridge and for white perch around the Key Bridge and Fort Howard. Access ramps include Broening Park in Middle Branch by the Hanover Street bridge; Merritt Point Park, Inverness Park, and Chesterwood Park, all on Bear Creek in Dundalk; and Fort Armistead Park at the south end of the Key Bridge. Call 410-887-3616 for information on all four.

The next river down is the Magothy, a short river with its watershed squeezed between Curtis, Stony, and Rock creeks, off the Patapsco to the north, and the Severn River to the south. Its headwaters are Lake Waterford, an Anne Arundel County Park. The Magothy is heavily settled, but it is interesting to explore with an outboard skiff, and you will find it well covered in cruise guides, especially areas like Sillery Bay and Dobbins Island on the north shore behind Gibson Island. Small boats will find some interesting headwater marshes in the creeks. The Magothy has good white perch and chain pickerel fishing. Look for the perch in spring and fall on submerged points and wrecks and pickerel in cold weather along the shore in the upper reaches. There is no public access, but several commercial marinas have launch ramps. Check the yellow pages in the Annapolis area telephone book and the ADC *Chartbook* for their names.

The Severn is a longer river, but it still functions as a tidal inlet. Its high banks have given it the nickname "the Hudson of the Chesapeake." It is especially pretty in afternoon light or with snow on its banks.

The Severn is also heavily settled, with heavy traffic on summer weekends. Even so, it has some good natural areas, especially a couple of creeks and several tidal ponds. In these areas, undisturbed soils in deep, wooded ravines produce consistent freshwater flows that result in small tidal fresh marshes growing behind brackish marshes. These areas provide small pockets of good habitat.

Even though virtually every creek has at least half a dozen houses, several are very attractive, including Luce, Clements, and Hopkins (behind St. Helena Island) on the south bank and Chase on the north. The head of the river (Severn Run) is also interesting, though it is shallow.

The best parts of the river are the tidal ponds, e.g., Martins, Rays, and Brewer. There is a shallow bar at the mouth of each, with deep water inside. Because of their bars, most boaters do not visit them. You will find if you proceed carefully, however, that you can get into each of them on virtually any tide in paddle/oar craft or an outboard skiff. Inside, you will find good marshes, both great blue and little green herons, waterfowl in season, and good perch fishing, especially around fallen trees. Access is tough, especially for paddle and oar craft. Truxtun Park in Annapolis (410-263-7958) and Sandy Point State Park (410-974-2149) are the only public launches, and there are only a couple of commercial marinas.

If you put overboard at Sandy Point State Park, you will have to run down around Hackett Point in the open Bay, but inside the point, you will find Whitehall Bay. While it is not technically part of the Severn, it is certainly a major feature of the Annapolis area, and it offers three interesting creeks for skiffs: Mill, Whitehall, and Meredith. Mill and Whitehall mix residences, marinas, and workboats. Meredith is strictly residential and beautiful, but the entrance is tight. Feel your way in carefully.

Like the Magothy and the Severn, the South River is heavily developed with houses and piers, and it has a number of commercial marinas as well. It is broad, and in warm weather, full of traffic. There are no public launch ramps, though several of the marinas have ramps open to the public. The ADC *Chartbook* can help.

Despite the traffic, the river has some beautiful creeks. Harness, for example, is bounded on one side by Anne Arundel County's new Quiet Waters Park (call 410-222-1777 for information on facilities). Other attractive creeks include Crab, Church, Broad, and Beards. The head of the river above Rt. 50 is silted in, but it is an interesting complex of little channels through marsh and swamp, worth exploring by canoe or kayak if you can find access.

The Rhode River benefits from having much of its watershed held by the Smithsonian Institution in outright ownership or easement, and a bit more by YMCA Camp Letts. Both Sellman Creek and Muddy Creek are interesting to paddle, but don't get out on shore without permission from the Smithsonian Environmental Research Center (410-798-4424) and

Camp Letts (410-798-0440). If you paddle up Muddy Creek within Smithsonian property, be very careful not to disturb scientific gear set in the water. Both of these creeks have shallow, muddy deltas that can be tricky to get over on low water even in a canoe, but there are nice brackish marshes inside. The Rhode River also has three islands, Big, Flat, and High. Look at each, and you will understand why they are named as they are. There is good access for paddle craft, rowboats, and light skiffs at the sand ramp of Carrs Wharf. Keep an eye out for an eagle over Muddy Creek. There has been a nest at the head of it for many years. If strong southerly winds are forecast, be very careful.

The West River is nice for exploring creeks and coves, especially to look at boats in the boat yards around Galesville. The headwaters of Lerch Creek behind Hartge Yacht Yard are also attractive. There is no public access except Galesville Park, which will allow you to launch a canoe or a kayak. You may also find one or two launch ramps at commercial marinas.

Trip Description: Gunpowder River

Type of Waterway—Tidal fresh

Directions and Access—Mariner Point Park (410-638-3570) at the end of Mariner Road, off Joppa Farm Road in Joppatowne. Put in and take out at Mariner Point Park.

Trip Routes—Paddle or run down the channel, around the corner, up into the Gunpowder's delta, and then into the river's main stem above.

Cautions—Be careful of powerboat traffic in the channel below the park. If you are in a canoe or kayak, stay out of the marked channel. The mouth of the delta is exposed to a strong southerly wind. Pick another spot if it is blowing.

Comments—This section of the Gunpowder looks today much different from the way it did even a hundred years ago. One could argue such a case for most of the Bay's tributaries, but changes in the Gunpowder are both well documented and quite pronounced; just above the delta, you'll find wharf pilings to which sailing vessels tied when they came to the port of Joppa Town in the 1700s. Today these posts are three miles from navigable water, and the port has not been active since 1768, when it was abandoned as the Baltimore County seat.

The port was abandoned because the river had filled in considerably. Signs of siltation are readily visible to today's explorer, and after a heavy rain the river's color is always brown.

Such background information about the river is not intended to discourage the visitor. Quite the contrary. The sediment, the history, and the geology of the river all provide good exploratory material. Piecing together the history and watching a silted river behave do have their advantages. The extensive Gunpowder marshes, for example, were created in large measure by land-use activities upstream; soil dislodged by logging, construction, and agriculture had to be deposited somewhere. Much of the turned over and exposed soil has been transported downstream by rainfall, and ultimately deposited in the lower river.

The delta is about two miles below the fall line of the Gunpowder. On another trip, without a boat, you may find it interesting to visit the Gunpowder Falls State Park (410-592-2897) and walk to the fall line. It is where the river's bed meets sea level and also the interface of one geologic region and another, specifically, the piedmont, which has hard weather-resistant rock subsoils, and the coastal plain, which is built on gravel, sand, and mud. The fall line is clearly marked by a large outcropping of granite schist (notice the high percentage of mica because it is visible downstream in the bottom sediments). The age of the schist can be traced to the Miocene epoch, perhaps 10 million years ago.

The portion of the river just above the delta boasts a floodplain ecosystem that in the spring is covered with wildflowers such as trout lilies and trillium. In the fall, it is full of migratory birds and pileated woodpeckers. The floodplain soils are very fertile because when the river leaves her channel during flood events to flow across the flat topography and expend her energy, new sediments are deposited.

During certain flood events in the past, drainage streams have developed along this floodplain. Although the ditches do not last long, the floodplain retains scars that are interesting to look into. They hold wooded wetlands with large populations of amphibians. Peepers and other tree frogs are especially audible in the spring when they conduct their mating antics.

Muskrats or signs of them are often found near these upland wooded marshes. They are herbivores, grazing on cattails, sedges, and other marsh plants. Although this upper section is strictly freshwater, the tidal amplitude is from one to two feet. Thus when the tide is low, entrances to muskrat dens are visible along the main stem.

By the time the Gunpowder flows down to the delta, the river has collected a watershed that stretches through Harford and Baltimore counties almost to Pennsylvania. Some of her waters have been lost to Baltimore's drinking supplies via Prettyboy and Loch Raven reservoirs, while others have been used to irrigate agricultural lands (41 percent of the land in the watershed is still agricultural).

As the floodplain widens out into the delta, you'll find a marshy area colonized primarily by cattails. This transformation is marked by a small marsh island. In his essay, "From a Blind on the Gunpowder Marsh" in *Birds and Marshes of the Chesapeake Bay Country*, Brooke Meanley describes this cattail habitat as "probably the best nesting substrate for such marsh dwellers as the red-winged blackbird, long-billed marsh wren, common gallinule, and least bittern." All four were common nesters during the 1930s. Today, every visitor will see a red-winged blackbird, many will see a marsh wren, the patient will see the bittern, and the very lucky and skilled will see the gallinule.

The island is also a landmark as far as the history of the river is concerned. When a modern map of the Gunpowder is compared to one dated 1780, it is clear that the most significant topographic changes are the water depth and the increase in marshland. The water depth at the island is two feet today; the island was the head of navigation then. A geographer in the 1940s estimated that in the fifty-one-year period between 1846 and 1897, an average of fifteen cubic feet per acre of sediment was deposited in the upper Gunpowder estuary. He further described the area: "Today . . . the scene at Joppa Town is one of desolation. Old foundations are still visible through the tangled growth of weeds and underbrush. At a distance of 20 or 30 feet out from the original shore line is a heap of stones, the remnants of the old wharf. A hundred feet beyond is tree-covered land where ships once rode at anchor." ("Effects of Soil Erosion on Navigation in Upper Chesapeake Bay," by L. C. Gottschalk, *Journal of Historical Geography,* 1946)

The delta marsh extends to the interface of the Bird and Gunpowder rivers. The Days Cove section on the northwest side is a highlight. The center portion is shallow, and not all parts are accessible to boats (even to canoes at low tide), but the depth at the opening is ten feet (look for catfish and perch), and the cove is well worth a careful visit.

Days Cove is distinguished by its birdlife. On a good fall day, a trip around it will flush up flocks of buffleheads, black ducks, coots, and geese, to name a few. The birds are generally found near the far shore (where there is a small patch of wild rice). In the spring and summer, great blue herons, green herons, sea gulls, and terns frequent the cove, but the numbers of birds are not as large as in the fall.

Perhaps the large flocks of waterfowl today are inconsequential compared to the flocks that fueled the market gunning industry until the 1920s. Then they were rumored to be three miles square and to blacken the sky. It is impossible to judge the accuracy of those stories, but it is a fact that the birds' food source, submerged aquatic grasses, have declined in the upper Bay–Susquehanna Flats region. Today, water milfoil (a less desirable food source) is found in small isolated patches, and choice grasses such as redhead pondweed and wild celery are quite rare.

The return to Mariner Point Park is a shock after Days Cove. The lower river joins the Bird River, whose banks at that point are covered with cottages. Many of these homes were built as summer cottages, and historically cottage communities such as these have contributed excess nutrients via their septic systems. The lower marsh is primarily phrag-mites (common reed), which is a less desirable marsh plant often asso-ciated with rapid siltation. The canal leading back to the park is a dredged waterway.

Modern Joppatowne was built in the 1960s, but like the old navigation channels upstream, it holds a place in history. The Gunpowder Cove development was built on reclaimed marshland. It could not be built today, since the Wetlands Protection Act of 1970 protects all tidal marshland.

I always end the trip with the same thoughts with which I began it, "I can't believe that that interesting river is tucked away behind this highway and suburb."

Patuxent River

The Patuxent is the longest river wholly within the state of Maryland, and it is the sixth-largest in the Bay system. It rises in the southeast corner of Frederick County and flows first southeast, then south through How-ard County, and then divides Prince George's County from Anne Arundel. The head of navigation in the seventheenth century was at Queen Anne Bridge, near Bowie, and its Western Branch made Upper Marlboro an important tobacco port. The poor soil conservation that the planters practiced as they cleared and farmed their land gradually filled the river with sand, gravel, and mud. Today only canoes call at Queen Anne Bridge and Upper Marlboro, and the river is navigable only to just above Hills Bridge (Rt. 4 at Waysons Corner).

More recently, intense suburban development in the Baltimore-Washington corridor, through which the upper river flows, has threatened its health. Poor sewage treatment, inadequate sediment control on building lots, and primitive washing operations at gravel pits along the upper river have damaged it severely all the way down to its mouth.

Over the past ten years, however, there has been a concentrated effort to solve those problems. The Patuxent now benefits from some of the best sewage treatment in the United States, and control of sediment from construction and gravel mining has been improved greatly. The river's water quality is beginning to turn around.

Situated where it is, in the midst of several million people, the Patuxent is a wonderful resource. Its tidal fresh section is as beautiful and rich as that of any other of the Bay's rivers. Its lower sections offer wonderful cruising ground for large boats, and its once-plentiful seafood resources now have a chance to rebound. The river is well worth the close attention of small boat explorers in the Baltimore-Washington area.

It is good and right that we work to care for the Patuxent as it flows through the midst of such a busy area. The river has been a highway for humans for thousands of years. Witness its name and the number of its tributary creeks with Native American names. At the same time, you will note that a number of other tributaries have English names. The river was settled early in the seventeenth century by Europeans and served as a highway for commercial vessels up until the 1930s, when the steamboats stopped running. During all those years, it provided valuable access to farms in what was otherwise a roadless area. Southern Maryland was a prosperous tobacco-growing area for the better part of four centuries, and for most of that time, the river was the best means to get the crop to market.

The Patuxent also served as a convenient back door to the city of Washington for anyone who did not wish to go up the Potomac. British Admiral Cockburn attempted to attack the nation's capital by this route during the War of 1812 but was prevented from doing so when U.S. Commander Joshua Barney scuttled his fleet to prevent Cockburn from making further progress up the river. Barney pulled off this defensive maneuver about one mile upstream of the mouth of Western Branch, or two miles above where Jug Bay is now. It is hard to imagine a major naval engagement in such a narrow freshwater stream today, but the site has been confirmed, and a vessel that probably belonged to Barney's fleet has been excavated by underwater archeologists.

Jug Bay itself is a bit of an anomaly. It does not show on maps drawn at the beginning of this century. There is speculation that it appeared after the railroad line from Washington to Chesapeake Beach was completed. The remains of this old line exist as a couple of caisson supports in midchannel just above Jackson's Landing and by the dike across the marsh just to the east of them that carried the railroad bed. This marsh is part of the Jug Bay Wetlands Sanctuary operated by Anne Arundel County (410-741-9330).

The Patuxent River Park, a property of the Maryland-National Capital Park and Planning Commission, was created in the early 1970s to give public access to the river. Since the steamboats stopped running on the river, this area has retained its rural character, in spite of its proximity to Washington and neighboring suburbs. The Park and Planning Commission sought to preserve this rural, natural character in the plans for the park. It is one of the finest public facilities in the Bay country. In addition to the launch ramps, it provides walking trails, campsites, and several excellent historical exhibits of life on the river in earlier times. Call 301-627-6075 for information.

The trip description below highlights one of our favorite waterways in the whole Bay system, Mattaponi Creek, but there are lots of others for people in small boats to explore, largely thanks to the efforts of the Maryland-National Capital Park and Planning Commission and Anne Arundel and Calvert counties' parks departments. In addition to Jug Bay, other good places include the river around Park and Planning's Magruder Landing boat ramp (ask the folks at the Patuxent River Park for details). Favorite spots in this section include Hall's Creek (just upriver), Terrapin Creek (which winds back into the big marsh opposite the old Magruder Landing steamboat wharf), and Cocktown Creek (just down-river, next to Calvert County's Kings Landing Park). All are suitable for canoes, kayaks, and outboard skiffs, but be careful in outboards of the bar at the mouth of each of the creeks.

Below Cocktown Creek, the river widens out, and, from Benedict down, it is a full-blown brackish tidal river, a mile or more in width. This is big-boat cruising territory, and the open river can get rough enough that nothing less than carefully piloted large outboard skiffs are safe. Some of the side creeks are great for poking around, and we have spent many a day in them with CBF's Maryland Canoe Fleet, but most of the access is private. There is a Calvert County launch ramp at Hallowing Point, opposite Benedict, and another at Solomons. Call the Calvert County parks department (410-535-1600) for information. You may also find a commercial ramp on Broomes Island. If you find a launch spot, by all means use it. A day on this part of the river is an excellent counterpoint to the tidal fresh section above.

In addition to the Patuxent River Park and the Jug Bay Wetlands Sanctuary, there are three other publicly owned facilities on the river well worth a visit, especially to gain historical perspective. They are the state's Jefferson Patterson Park (410-586-8500) at the mouth of St. Leonard Creek, the wonderful Calvert Marine Museum at Solomons (410-326-2042), and Calvert County's Battle Creek Cypress Swamp Sanctuary (410-535-5327).

Trip Description: Mattaponi Creek

Type of Waterway—Tidal fresh

Directions and Access—Mattaponi Creek is located approximately twenty miles east of Washington, D.C., near Upper Marlboro, off Rt. 301. Contact the Patuxent River Park (301-627-6074) for information and directions. The park maintains excellent launching ramps at Jackson's Landing (next to the park office) and at Selby's Landing just downriver. Both are suitable for launching paddle and row craft and powerboats up to twenty feet. For those desiring a one-way trip by canoe or kayak, the park can arrange for a shuttle to its put-in at Queen Anne Bridge ten miles upstream. There is much to be said, however, for careful exploration of the immediate area before making the trip down from Queen Anne Bridge.

Trip Routes—If you can spend several days in the area, we strongly recommend exploring the river and the broad expanse of Jug Bay, which extends between Jackson's Landing and Selby's Landing. Two interesting tributaries are Western Branch, a half-mile upstream from Jackson's Landing, and Mattaponi Creek, a quarter-mile downstream from Selby's Landing. If you have no particular destination in mind, consider the tide and choose accordingly between these two alternatives. If you have a powerboat, by all means explore the main stem of the river above Western Branch and also below Selby's Landing. Lyons Creek, on the opposite side of the river just below the mouth of Mattaponi, is also an interesting creek, and the big marsh just below it on the Mattaponi Creek side has several narrow, twisting guts that are well worth side trips. If you have to pick only one area, choose Mattaponi Creek.

Cautions—Tides are strong on the main stem of the river, and winds can be variable as well. If you are paddling or rowing, be conservative about making headway into either one. Jug Bay is much shallower than the main stem of the river and wide open enough to catch a good deal of wind. If you're in a powerboat, be careful of drifting onto a mud flat too shallow to navigate.

Comments—Of all the places to explore around the Patuxent River Park, Mattaponi Creek is a special favorite. Put overboard and take out at Selby's Landing. If you have a minnow seine, pull it on the sandbars on either side of the pier and launch ramp. There are a number of small fish in there almost anytime. In late summer and fall, you may catch as many as fifteen species, some of them totally local residents like bass and sunfish right beside others that have come all the way from the continental shelf, like young spot and menhaden.

As you paddle down the river toward the creek mouth, notice first the old wharf pilings 100 yards below the boat ramp. They are invisible on a high tide but show up at most other stages. Be sure to avoid running into them, no matter what kind of boat you are in, but let them remind you that right up to the beginning of the twentieth century, farmers shipped their produce to market via the river.

Just before you get to the creek mouth, you will see the remains of an old barge on the right-hand bank, nestled back into a cove against a stand of common reed grass. This is the *Peter Cooper*, a steam barge that was used to build the Chesapeake Beach railroad line. If you are fishing, it is worth making a cast or two to the eddies that form around the barge on both incoming and outgoing tides. Note, however, that the timbers and spikes on the barge will foul your line. Choose your bait accordingly and make sure that you keep your boat away from the barge. It extends out into the river for sixty or seventy feet.

There is a bar at the mouth of the creek. As happens on a number of the Bay's tidal fresh waterways, a creek coming into a river's main stem on the outside of a curve will deposit a sand bar, pushing the channel from the outside of the turn into the middle. The river channel out in the middle is twenty feet deep, while the mouth of Mattaponi Creek is only three to four feet. Right inside the creek, the channel drops back down to nine feet and then comes back up to three very quickly. Sometimes in the spring, white and yellow perch will congregate in this hole. There is another deep hole (fifteen feet deep) just a little farther upstream, where a small gut comes out of the marsh on the left-hand side.

Bass and catfish will lie at the upstream edge of this hole, waiting for food that is swept down into it by the tide.

In October and November, this stretch of the creek often has large concentrations of waterfowl on it. The marsh is high-quality mixed tidal fresh vegetation, with lots of wild rice, smartweed, and tearthumb.

If you have a depth-sounder, watch it as you paddle up the creek. It will show you all sorts of bars and holes. After several more turns up the creek, there is a small landing for the Merkle Wildlife Management Area which is operated by the state. Check with the personnel at Patuxent River Park about access to this landing before using it. If you are on the creek in waterfowl season, check also with park personnel about duck hunters. There is one blind on the creek, and one family that retains gunning rights. Normally it is easy to work around their schedule, but it is best to deal with this issue in advance.

Above the landing, the creek becomes shallower, with a sandier bottom, as it extends up into an extensive wooded watershed. A quarter-mile above the landing, Mattaponi flows past a high wooded bank on the Merkle side, with a large marsh on the park side. There is a bridge across this stretch of the creek that was built to provide driving access.

Another quarter-mile above is a substantial beaver dam that has been there for a dozen years. If you are in a powerboat, this is the end of the line. If you are in a canoe, and if the tide is up, you may be able to slide your boat over the dam and continue upstream. The creek at this point begins to disappear into the woods, and shrubs and trees appear along the bank with increasing frequency. One of the reasons for the beaver dam is that there is an abundance of alders, stream bank shrubs that are a particularly favorite food of beavers. Wood ducks nest in this area, and the pool behind the dam is used by other waterfowl in the early spring and in the fall.

In spite of the fact that much of the region around Mattaponi Creek is in farmland, wooded banks protect the waterway from heavy silt runoff. Even at times when heavy rains cloud the main stem of the Patuxent, Mattaponi will run clear. Exploring the upper reaches will give you an excellent opportunity to observe the value of trees in protecting creeks and rivers from heavy runoff. It is always a shock for us in this upper portion of the creek, which feels very wild, to realize that we are less than twenty miles as the goose flies from the U.S. Capitol in Washington.

Mattaponi Creek offers some good fishing opportunities. A light spinning rod with a small plastic-tailed grub jig is an excellent choice for the variety of white perch, yellow perch, crappie, largemouth bass, and channel catfish that live there. The fish live by the tide, using fallen trees and other obstructions as current breaks and ambush points. Just above the landing, for example, there is a large stump in midstream. Cast your bait past it and swim it back close to the stump, always moving it *with* the tide. If you are primarily interested in catfish, it is a wise move to fish earthworms on the bottom in the deep holes that you find with a sonar or leadline.

One final note: Mattaponi Creek is host to several thousand visitors a year. No waterway can withstand this kind of traffic unless the people who use it treat it with extreme care. The Patuxent River Park has very strict rules about debris of any sort. Be careful of what you bring in and take out. If you find someone else's trash, by all means take it with you. If you fish, take only what you need and put back anything else you catch. Mattaponi has survived this far because of the care that people before you have given it. Please keep the chain going and pass the favor on to those coming behind you.

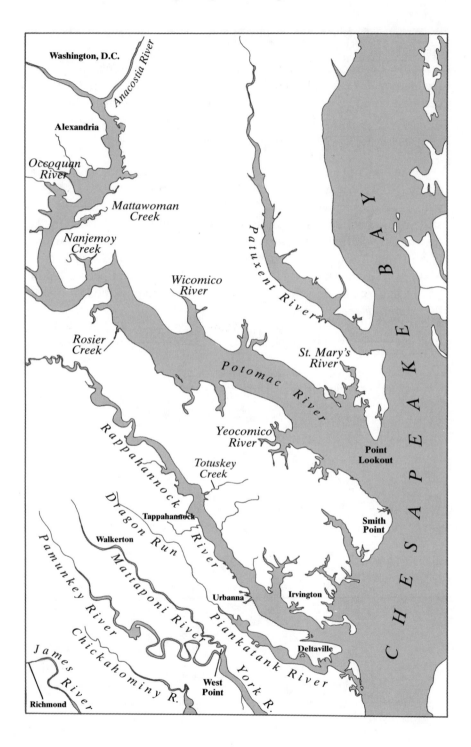

Washington, D.C.

Anacostia River

Alexandria

Occoquan
River

Mattawoman
Creek

Nanjemoy
Creek

Wicomico
River

Patuxent River

B
A
Y

Rosier
Creek

Potomac River

St. Mary's
River

C
H
E
S
A
P
E
A
K
E

Rappahannock

Yeocomico
River

Totuskey
Creek

Point
Lookout

Dragon Run

Tappahannock

Walkerton

Mattaponi River

Rappahannock River

Smith
Point

Pamunkey River

Chickahominy

Urbanna

Piankatank River

Irvington

Deltaville

James
River

Chickahominy R.

West
Point

York R.

Richmond

nine

Potomac River

The Potomac is a major river unto itself, the eighth largest on the Atlantic Coast of the United States. One of the remarkable features of the Susquehanna/Chesapeake system is the number of big tributaries that empty into the tidal portion of it. The Potomac is the largest of these. Just for comparison, it carries about 40 percent as much fresh water as the Susquehanna.

The Potomac's rich history is part of its identity. Native Americans fished and hunted along it for some eight thousand years before European settlement in the first half of the seventeenth century. Then rich soils and plenty of deep tributary creeks combined to form a prosperous resource for the decentralized agrarian economy of the time, with each plantation able to have its own wharf. The river's hundred miles of navigable waters penetrated deep into the Maryland and Virginia colonies, so it was natural that port cities should spring up near the head of navigation at Georgetown, Alexandria, and Bladensburg (on the Anacostia, a major subtributary). This access to ports helped to open up the settlement of Western Maryland and Virginia's Shenandoah Valley.

The colonists also discovered early that the Potomac was a great fishing river, especially when shad, herring, sturgeon, and rockfish ran up to spawn during late March, April, and May. The fishermen cleared hundreds of "stands" for haul seines. These were broad flats in the river which they swept free of tree stumps and other obstructions washed in on spring floods. The seines were long nets that were stretched from shore by large rowboats carrying as many as a dozen oarsmen. One of these seine skiffs would pull its end of the net in a semicircle across the flat and bring it back into shore near the other end that had been anchored there. With whatever fish were on the flat thus trapped in the net, the fishing crew pulled it into the beach. Shad were caught by the thousands, herring by the tens of thousands. They were eaten fresh or salted for market. Sturgeon ran six to ten feet in length and sometimes even more. They were often smoked. Rockfish ran very large, with a number exceeding fifty pounds in weight. George Washington was one of the most serious practitioners of these spring haul seine fisheries. He considered fishing an important profit center for his plantation, Mount Vernon.

Much of the character of the Potomac was captured by Frederick Tilp over forty years of cruising and sixty years of researching it. See his book *This Was Potomac River* for a detailed expansion of the ideas above, including firsthand descriptions of life on the river just as the age of freight under sail was ending in the 1930s and '40s.

As so often happens to great natural resources, the Potomac River attracted enough people to cause it pollution problems. The river's capacity for transportation opened up the Maryland and Virginia piedmont and the fertile Shenandoah Valley to agriculture. As has been noted above, early colonial agriculture paid scant heed to soil conservation, and, as on other river systems, this caused terrible sediment problems on the Potomac. By the early eighteenth century, the merchants of the city of Alexandria were concerned that the channel to their port city was silting in. The channel to Bladensburg on the Anacostia filled in at an even more alarming rate. Today the upper reaches of that river are completely blocked to any but the most shallow-draft vessels. The main stem of the Potomac continues to experience problems with siltation.

As the nation's capital grew in the late nineteenth and early twentieth centuries, the city of Washington began to pollute the Potomac to a serious degree with sewage. In the 1960s, Lyndon Johnson called the river "a national disgrace." Help came from the Clean Water Act of 1972 and a determination to make the city's sewage treatment a national showcase. The D.C. Blue Plains Sewage Treatment Plant, once a source of the river's problems, developed an excellent advanced wastewater treatment system with superior phosphorous control.

The river has seen tremendous improvement in the last twenty years, including great resurgence of submerged aquatic vegetation, a sensitive indicator of water quality. Much of this vegetation is an introduced species, hydrilla, but that grass has proven to be highly beneficial to the river, in spite of the fact that a number of commercial and community marinas must have their channels "mowed" several times each season to keep them open. Several other native species are doing reasonably well also, including wild celery, coontail, and water star grass. There is a small Eurasian clam that has multiplied in the soft sediments of the river and now plays a major role in clarifying the waters as well. The improved water quality and the habitat value provided by the grasses have led to a strong resurgence of fish and waterfowl on the river. The birdlife is exciting in all seasons, and the area has developed into one of the finest fisheries for largemouth bass in the country, with over twenty professional guides currently active. See Ken Penrod's book *Fishing the Tidal Potomac River* for details.

The Potomac is not out of the woods by any means, however. Blue Plains is not yet doing nitrogen removal, which will be necessary to help the lower river make as dramatic an improvement as the upper river. The lower river has improved somewhat because basic treatment at Blue Plains helps, as do recent efforts to reduce agricultural runoff and improve local sewage treatment. As in other parts of the Bay system, however, the oyster beds are in trouble, and the food fishery in the lower river is less productive than it was in earlier years, especially for spot and croakers. Shad, herring, and sturgeon stocks are still depressed, but the rockfish population is rebounding.

No river with over two million people in its watershed is ever safe from damage, and there is a great deal yet to do to bring the Potomac back to its former glory. Still, its progress is something to celebrate. It is a big, beautiful river with lots of interesting areas to explore.

The Upper Tidal Potomac: Washington, D.C., to Morgantown

The Potomac is tidal fresh from Little Falls down to Quantico. Throughout this whole stretch, it is very powerful, and above Mount Vernon it is quite capable of rising out of its banks on a spring flood. Look at the shoreline anywhere along this area, and you will see a river floodplain with narrow sand beaches, lots of driftwood, and wet-ground trees like sycamores and maples. Above Memorial Bridge and the Kennedy Center, currents are powerful, even in times of low rainfall, so canoeists, kayakers, and rowers should be especially careful. Below that point, the main river is wider and more suitable to outboard skiffs. A big river like this, however, forms island and shoals with the sediments it carries, so it is laced with creek mouths and backwater sloughs. These are good areas for paddle/oar craft. Much of the river's shore belongs to the National Park Service, with private concessionaires operating the facilities.

The access farthest upriver is Fletchers Boat House (202-244-0461), between Chain Bridge and Little Falls. The same family has operated this facility for two generations, and they know the river well, especially the fishing and how to be safe. They rent wooden skiffs for rowing or for small outboards that their customers bring to clamp onto them.

Just above the Kennedy Center, Thompson Boat Center (202-333-4861) provides access for cartop boats and serves several rowing clubs in the area. This is a logical spot for exploring the Georgetown waterfront and Theodore Roosevelt Island just across the water. A six-knot speed limit is vigorously enforced. Be careful of floodwaters and especially of floating debris. Try to picture the Georgetown waterfront 150 years ago, with schooners at anchor in this curve of the river.

From Theodore Roosevelt Island downriver to Mount Vernon, the Virginia shore is almost entirely public land (with the exception of Washington National Airport and the City of Alexandria). It is well worth driving, biking, running, and walking in any season. These are all legitimate forms of river exploration but are normally not available when riverbanks are privately owned. The D.C. shoreline may be explored in similar fashion from Rock Creek Park down past Thompson's to West Potomac and East Potomac parks. Carry binoculars and scan the river to learn from it, just as you would if afloat.

Below Memorial Bridge, the Potomac is big boat water, best for outboard skiffs from sixteen to twenty feet. Be careful of traffic, especially tour boats, and of the stiff chop that builds in winds of twelve knots or more. Also notice that the channel winds back and forth, with shallow shoals on both sides. In warm weather, submerged aquatic vegetation will mark some of these shoals, but even then its presence or absence is no substitute for prudence.

The Anacostia deserves special mention. As noted, Bladensburg was once a major port, responsible for opening up much of what is now western Prince George's County. The headwaters of the river are in the piedmont. As also is noted above, in Chapter 8, streams that originate in the piedmont are very susceptible to siltation. One look at a map of the Anacostia below Bladensburg will remind you of the Gunpowder delta. There are lots of islands and back channels. Put overboard at Anacostia Park (202-561-5388) and paddle, row, or run (six-knot limit, vigorously enforced) one to two miles up into the delta. The Chesapeake Bay Foundation is just beginning to use this area for field trips. Some of the river is sad-looking, full of trash, but there are interesting pockets of wild rice and other plants, plus some good birding. The Anacostia has not made as much progress as the Potomac. There are still major problems with sewer overflows and stormwater runoff, but interest is high in cleaning it up. It may see significant progress by the turn of the century.

Around and below the Woodrow Wilson Bridge, there is good fishing, especially in Smoot Bay, an old gravel pit that now provides excellent spawning and year-round living habitat for largemouth bass. Ken Penrod's book has an extensive section on this part of the river. On the Virginia shore just below the bridge, the Belle Haven Marina (703-768-0018) is a good facility for launching skiffs and paddle/oar craft. Explore the back channels from the marina downriver to Dyke Marsh. This is a good area for marshes, birds, and fish. You will also note a crew of watermen working channel catfish in the area. The only problem with Belle Haven is that it is crowded on warm weather weekends.

Below Belle Haven, there are many other access points. On the Maryland side, consider especially Fort Washington Marina (301-292-7700) and the National Colonial Farm (301-283-2113) on Piscataway Creek. General Smallwood State Park on Mattawoman Creek (301-743-7613) is another good facility, and Mattawoman offers excellent bass fishing.

Note the contrast between Piscataway and Mattawoman creeks on the Maryland side and the creeks on the Virginia side. Piscataway and Mattawoman are coastal plain streams and behave in much the same way that rivers on the Eastern Shore do. On the Virginia side, creeks like Accotink, Pohick, Occoquan, and Quantico all drain piedmont land. Old U.S. Rt. 1 and Interstate 95 here lie approximately on the fall line. Each of these streams rises well to the west of those two highways but becomes tidal almost immediately on running underneath them. For an example of the results, put overboard at Pohick Bay Regional Park (703-339-6104) and make your way across to the delta in Accotink Bay. (On the way, respect the prohibitions around the docks at the Army Corps of Engineers' Fort Belvoir.) The Accotink delta is now *very* shallow, yet in the second half of the nineteenth century, a shipyard two miles upstream from this point (near the current U.S. Rt.1 crossing) built a number of schooners and an early steamboat. Think about that yard if you try to paddle over the delta. Accotink drains land well up in the center of Fairfax County. Agriculture and development over the past ninety years have sent a tremendous amount of sand, gravel, and mud down the creek. The marshes of the delta are good ones, but the creek's overall habitat value has definitely been reduced.

The Mason Neck State Park between Pohick Bay and Occoquan Bay is well worth a visit on foot. Call 703-550-0960 for information. The refuge has an extensive mature hardwood forest with streams and beaver ponds draining to a big tidal fresh marsh on the river. There are deer, wild turkeys, and especially eagles. Keep an eye out for them in the refuge or out on the river.

The Occoquan River is also well worth a visit. Read Tilp on the history of the town and Penrod on the fishing. In brief, the Occoquan River drains a large piedmont watershed, so the town that grew up at the fall line was well suited for shipping and had waterpower for early industrial development. It is now partially restored and interesting to visit. There are many big boat marinas, but small boats can launch at Occoquan Regional Park (703-690-2121). Be careful of traffic on the river, but do explore. You will notice a sewage treatment plant upriver. The plants on the Occoquan are generally well-run, state-of-the-art installations that help to maintain its health.

Below Occoquan and Mattawoman, the Potomac is wide, not really small boat territory except in the side creeks. Quantico Creek is interesting, although it is very shallow, and there is no public access. Like Joppa Town on the Gunpowder, the old port city of Dumfries has been completely silted in.

Some ten miles farther down, the river begins a long dogleg turn that marks the transistion to its lower reaches. On the Virginia side are Aquia and Potomac creeks, and on the Maryland side, Nanjemoy and Port Tobacco, all interesting and full of history. There is good public access on Nanjemoy (see the trip description below). There are commercial marinas in Aquia Creek and the Port Tobacco River. Virginia's Caledon State Park is a major eagle roost, well worth a visit. Call 540-663-3722 for information. Also keep an eye out for the birds whenever you are on that part of the river.

Trip Description: Nanjemoy Creek

Type of Waterway—Tidal fresh/brackish creek

Directions and Access—Public boat ramp at Friendship Landing (301-870-3388). From Rt. 301 in La Plata take Rt. 6 west to the village of Ironsides and turn south (left) onto Rt. 425. After about $2\frac{1}{2}$ miles, turn left onto Friendship Landing Road and drive one mile to ramp at end.

Trip Routes—There is more than a day's worth of exploring here, even in a powerboat. The standard trip is five miles up the main stem of the creek and back down, but the marshes of the lower creek hold eagles, ospreys, herons, and waterfowl, and the heads of Burgess Creek and Hill Top Fork offer fine marshes as well.

Cautions—If you venture below Friendship Landing in a small boat, be careful if the winds are over ten knots—the lower part of Nanjemoy is shallow, and any strong wind can build a nasty chop that you'll have to fight going or coming. Also, pay close attention to channel markers on the lower creek and exercise prudence upstream in wider areas where the creek shoals up. On the upper creek, there are submerged logs and a boat wreck (it is buoyed) that can damage an outboard motor.

Comments—In the mid-seventeenth century, early members of the Dent family built a house here and named it, the landing beside it, and their ship Friendship (information from Tilp). Think about the location as you put overboard. It's a natural: a deep hole next to a wooded bank at a location where a large, navigable creek narrows down to a tiny harbor, just right for a colonial ship. The Dents farmed and probably timbered the land, and they fished the creek.

In July 1931, Tilp and his Sea Scouts sailed up Nanjemoy Creek, "passing many fish traps and three long boats and barges loading pulp wood. Ashore at Friendship Landing, talked to Mr. Arthur Karlson and his wife Rita, who worked a farm, shipping wheat and pulp wood to Alexandria: averaging over 1,000 cords a year. Trapping muskrats seems to be the best business during winter season." (p. 256)

Today, Friendship Landing is a public facility, but nearby landowners are still farming and cutting pulpwood, and the creek's marshes are full of muskrat lodges. The surrounding country is still rural, despite the rapid suburbanization of the rest of Charles County. Nanjemoy's primary notoriety today is its bass fishery. Anglers come from far and wide to work its fallen trees and grass beds for largemouths. They also find rockfish, catfish, pickerel, white perch, yellow perch, and crappie. Aside from fishing boat traffic, however, you will find the creek beautiful and uncrowded.

As noted above, the lower part of Nanjemoy is wide, a poor place for a canoe or a kayak, but the headwaters of its two major side branches, Burgess Creek and Hill Top Fork, are well worth exploring. Keep an eye out for all sorts of birds, especially ospreys, eagles, great blue herons, and waterfowl. There is a major heron rookery in the wooded swamp at the head of Burgess Creek that is preserved by the Maryland Chapter of The Nature Conservancy. You can't get a boat up the creek that far, but you'll see plenty of herons in the area because of the rookery.

The main stem of Nanjemoy Creek winds west, then south, for more than five miles, and you can explore nearly all of it in a small boat, though any skiff over sixteen feet will have a difficult time in the extreme headwaters. The marshes at Friendship Landing are brackish, but they give way gradually to tidal fresh vegetation. About three miles up, the channel divides to form several islands, with nice back channels behind them, and then the creek turns into a tunnel of wooded swamp, running between alders and ironwood trees on the banks, with hugh mature oaks just behind them. Keep an eye out for water birds of all sorts, including eagles.

Read Ken Penrod on the fishing and Fred Tilp on the history. Take your binoculars, field guides, camera, and tackle. Go explore Nanjemoy. It is one of the Chesapeake's best.

The Lower Potomac River: Morgantown to Smith Point

Below Morgantown and the U.S. Rt. 301 bridge, the river changes again. Now it is big and wide, and getting salty. Although crabs travel all the way up to Washington, they are most abundant in this part of the river, and the oyster beds begin about at Morgantown. The land on each side of the river takes on a special character, Southern Maryland to the north and the Northern Neck of Virginia to the south. This region is largely rural, out of the sphere of daily influence of the Washington Metropolitan Area. The open river is suitable only for big skiffs and larger vessels, but there are many interesting side creeks. Again, read Tilp's book for historical commentary, especially the chapter, "A Sea Scout Cruise," in which he and his mates visited virtually every creek, wharf, store, and fishing village on the tidewater river on a four-week trip in 1931. It is an extraordinary picture of life on the river in a not-so-distant time. The standard cruise guides also cover most of this area well. What follows is a scattering of suggestions for up-the-creek areas that those guides miss.

The largest "creek" in this area (where all tidal tributaries are so classified by local people) is the Wicomico River (not to be confused with the one of the same name on the Eastern Shore at Salisbury, or the other two down at the end of the Northern Neck). This river drains Zekiah

Swamp. There is good access at Chaptico and Bushwood wharves (301-863-6068), both old steamboat landings. The open Wicomico is best for skiffs, but you may be able to work out access at the head of the river for paddle/oar craft. The interface between Zekiah and the Wicomico is called Allens Fresh Run. It is an interesting mix of tidal fresh and brackish habitat. The Wicomico below is rich in the history of finfish and shellfish harvesting, especially white perch, rockfish, oysters, and crabs.

Three other creeks, St. Clements Bay, Breton Bay, and the St. Mary's River, join the river on the Maryland side. All are rural in character, with a strong heritage of commercial fishing, boatbuilding, and farming. The region is struggling today to convert from tobacco to more profitable crops. A public launch ramp in Leonardtown provides good access to McIntosh Run, an interesting little woodland stream that feeds Breton Bay. The St. Mary's River is very pretty and easy to explore by canoe or kayak from the roadside near St. Mary's College in St. Mary's City. Be careful, though, about parking in restricted areas. Paddle up past Tippity Witchity Island and through the delta to the upper river. If the wind is strong, explore Fisherman Creek by the college. Access for skiffs is available downriver at the Piney Point Recreation Area and the St. Inigoes Recreation Area (301-863-6068).

On the Virginia side, there is a series of medium and small creeks all worth visiting. Rosier Creek near Colonial Beach is a CBF favorite, tidal fresh at the head but strongly brackish at the mouth, only a mile and a half below. There is no public access, but if you scout around Rt. 205 at Potomac Beach just upriver from Colonial Beach, you may find a place where you can get permission to put a canoe or a kayak overboard. Upper Machodoc Creek (just above Rosier) and Mattox Creek (just below Colonial Beach) are longer but basically like Rosier: good places to explore in a skiff. Use Colonial Beach Landing (804-367-1000) to launch.

Nomini Creek is beautiful. Hollis Marsh, a barrier island just outside, is beautiful but private and posted. Don't go on it without permission, but feel free to paddle or idle along it to look at the birds, especially ospreys. Tide rips and marsh banks around the island might favor you with rockfish if you fish them in season. The brackish upper creek is well worth exploring in a skiff. For access, look for a commercial marina at Coles Point on Lower Machodoc Creek, which is also worth exploring. Coles Point has been a center for watermen for years.

Below Coles Point are three short creeks, Gardner, Jackson, and Bonum. Access to Gardner and Jackson is tough but possible by skiff from Bonum. Bonum Creek has a nice ramp (804-367-1000) that will accommodate both skiffs and paddle/oar craft. It is a couple of miles long, just right for a leisurely paddle on a pretty day. There are some nice marshes at the headwaters. You will find herons and ospreys, and if you hunt carefully, some nice white perch.

The next river down, the Yeocomico, has much to offer. It is described below.

Beyond the Yeocomico is the Coan River, another good one. Look for a commercial marina at Lewisetta to launch and explore the Coan itself and its tributary, The Glebe. Between the Yeocomico and the Coan, there is enough to see to spend a week, especially if you read up on the two rivers' history as well.

The river shore down to Smith Point has a series of short creeks with shallow mouths and no public access. All of them, however, are interesting if you can get into them.

At the mouth of the Potomac on the Virginia side, at Smith Point, is the Little Wicomico ("Little River"). It is a very interesting area. Watermen have lived on it for years, but because Smith Point is so exposed to the weather from the north, the west, and the east, the mouth of the Little Wicomico has had a long history of shifting around. After the 1933 hurricane, which played havoc with it, the Corps of Engineers dredged an inlet at the tip of Smith Point and stabilized it with tons and tons of granite riprap. The riprap provides interesting habitat, the closest thing to a Maine tidepool that you will see on the Chesapeake. As the tides roar in and out of the inlet, they dig a large washout hole (fifteen feet deep) just outside. Controlling depth in the inlet is about five feet, but the currents shift sand back and forth, so it is treacherous for keel boats. It is also no place for canoes, kayaks, or rowing skiffs, especially because at times it is busy with powerboat traffic. It is no problem, however, for a well-powered outboard skiff and well worth fishing for a variety that includes flounder, bluefish, rockfish, gray trout, and sometimes "puppy drum" (young channel bass).

The best way to study Smith Point in detail, however, whether by skiff or paddle/oar craft, is to get permission to explore Kohls Island, which is owned by the Virginia Outdoors Foundation. Call 804-225-2147 for information. Use a commercial marine facility like Smith Point Marina to launch and run or paddle across to the old river mouth at the western end of the island. It shows up as a cove that nearly cuts Kohls Island off from the river shore. Pull your boat up into the marsh and walk the beach down to the rocks at the inlet. Be very careful if you climb on the rocks that you don't slip and fall. By all means look around at the creatures growing on the rocks and in the tide pools, but be careful not to cut your hands as you handle the rocks. Be sure to explore the marshes on the back side of the island as you work your way back to your boat, though you should beware of chiggers in season in the pine woods next to the marshes. If you are in an outboard, you can explore the upper part of the Little Wicomico as well. You will find lots of workboats, a public car ferry at Sunnybank, and a major fleet of charter fishing boats. The Little Wicomico offers more of the lower Potomac at its best.

Trip Description: Yeocomico River

Type of Waterway—Brackish river

Comments—The Yeocomico is home waters for me, the creek that taught me to love marshes. It spreads in all directions, a great place for a kid in a skiff and not bad for the judicious use of canoes, kayaks, and row-boats. Lodge Landing (804-367-1000), an old steamboat wharf on Lodge Creek (the south arm of the Yeocomico), offers a launch ramp. Be careful of powerboat traffic, but there is a lot to explore here, including tidal fresh marshes at the head of Lodge and Mill creeks. Some big white perch (locally called "grey perch," or "stiffbacks") swim in these seldom-visited upper creeks. The village of Harryhogan in between Lodge and Mill creeks houses the Krentz Marine Railway, an important facility that built one of the last working skipjacks now dredging oysters under sail (the *H. M. Krentz*) and regularly does repairs on a number of the other boats still operating in the fleet.

Several commercial marinas on other arms of the creek allow access to Kinsale, the oldest town on the Virginia side of the Potomac (founded 1706). Tilp, as usual, has plenty to say about Kinsale, including a brief description of a battle that took place in the War of 1812. The town is in many ways just as it was fifty years ago, except that one of its general stores is long since closed and the other one has a difficult time staying in business now. During steamboat days, there was a hotel here, but that is long gone as well. The old steamboat wharf at the foot of the hill still serves a couple of grain elevators where wheat and corn grown on neighboring farms are shipped out by a couple of small freighters still operating out of Deltaville.

Just to the south of Kinsale is Hampton Hall Branch, a nice long creek for paddling or rowing. If the tide is up, you may have to portage the bridge for Rt. 202, but above the bridge the creek turns to tidal fresh and runs through small rice marshes into a woodland.

My favorite marina on the Yeocomico is Earl Jenkins's Sandy Point Marina (804-472-3237). Earl has an adequate launch ramp for skiffs up to twenty feet, a small marine railway, and a store that sells almost everything you can think of. It is as nice a country boatyard as you will find. Ask Earl about his years of hauling lumber under sail on the schooner *Mattie F. Dean.*

There are brackish coves all around for exploring by paddle and oar, and Earl's is a perfect jumping-off point for exploring the Yeocomico in a skiff. There are at least half a dozen short creeks and coves worth exploring beyond the ones described above.

ten

The Rappahannock River
and the Northern Neck Bayshore Creeks

The Northern Neck of Virginia has had an identity all its own for nearly four hundred years. Home of great plantations and birthplace of presidents (Washington and Monroe), it was called "the Athens of America" during the early eighteenth century. Lying between the Potomac and Rappahannock rivers, laced with long tidal creeks, it was ideally suited for the agrarian society under which the Bay country flourished for years. Today it is still agrarian and rural, and just far enough from Washington, D.C., Baltimore, and Richmond to have received less pressure than Southern Maryland and the upper Eastern Shore. There is a great deal of second home and retirement development, but there are still many good areas to explore. That last statement, by the way, is roughly true also for the south bank of the Rappahannock, whose history is parallel. These lands are the backdrop for the waterways considered here.

The Bayshore creeks at the eastern end of the Northern Neck around the corner from the Little Wicomico are all beautiful and interesting brackish water areas, well worth exploring. They are deep enough that they are covered in the cruise guides, but as usual, not at the uppermost ends. The easiest one to get into is the Great Wicomico. Use Coopers Landing (804-367-1000) between Burgess and Wicomico Church on Rt. 200 to launch and explore in both directions. The head of the creek has some tidal fresh areas, but most of it is brackish. Both paddle/oar craft and skiffs are appropriate. In a larger skiff, explore downriver as well,

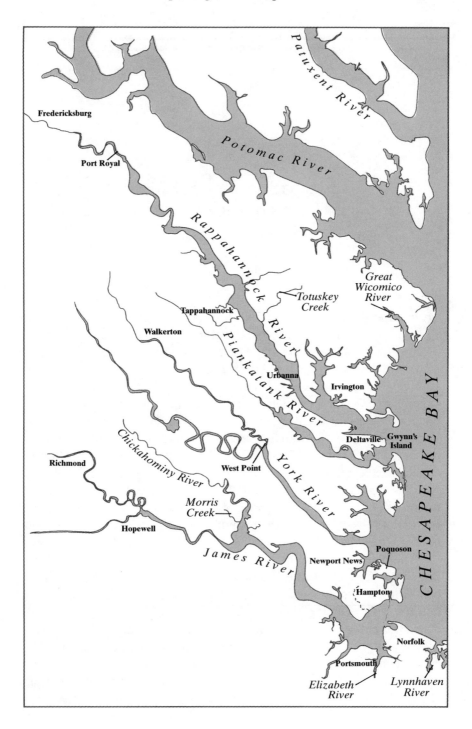

and, if you are interested in fish, work the pilings of the Glebe Point bridge for white perch and rockfish.

It is also interesting to explore Reedville, especially if you look at the history of its menhaden fishery. Menhaden (also called bunkers in Virginia and alewives in Maryland) are herring relatives, bony but very oily. The oil is used for industrial purposes (paint, cosmetics, tempering steel, and a host of other applications), with the high protein meal that is left over after cooking being used for chicken feed. Reedville is one of the largest American fishing ports, with an average of 400 million pounds landed per year. The fishery is highly mechanized, with some twenty 120-foot ships ("steamers"), forty 26-foot purse boats, and half a dozen airplanes (for spotting fish) involved in it. The menhaden fishery is a major source of employment for the Northern Neck.

Menhaden are fascinating fish that filter plankton and decayed plant material out of the water to feed on. These sources give them a vast food base, large enough to sustain the industrial fishery, provide another 150 million pounds of crab bait throughout the Bay each year, allow the menhaden to serve as forage fish for virtually every predator in the Bay from bluefish to largemouth bass, and leave enough to reproduce the species. To study the menhaden, read John Frye's *The Men All Singing*, visit the Waterman's Museum in Reedville, and put a skiff overboard at Shell Landing (804-367-1000) on Cockrell's Creek between Reedville and the village of Fleeton to explore the area.

The other creeks at the end of the Northern Neck, especially Dividing, Indian, and Dymer, are all attractive and interesting, but they have no public access. You may, however, be able to find commercial access by checking with boat dealers in Kilmarnock.

The Rappahannock River's history developed in much the same way as the Potomac's, except that the Rappahannock is smaller and doesn't reach as far back into the mountains. The river begins on the eastern slopes of the Blue Ridge as two arms, the main stem to the north and the Rapidan to the south. The Tidewater portions were settled first, of course, and a port town (Fredericksburg) grew up at the head of navigation. Settlers moved upstream to farm the rich piedmont soils, so Fredericksburg thrived as a port for years and still retains some of the character of a colonial town, though other business keeps it going today.

While Fredericksburg has always taken good care of its colonial houses, like Kenmore (which is open to the public), it neglected its waterfront for years, and sewage and industrial waste damaged the river, as did soil erosion from piedmont farms. Those first two problems are much improved now, but farm runoff can still cause damage. Also a problem now is pressure for development for commuters to the Washington Metropolitan Area and to Richmond; this is changing the character of the watershed.

Even so, the city is reviving its riverfront. There is a new City Dock Park with two good boat ramps on Sophia Street, and there are several areas available for walking the riverbank. Paddle/oar craft can explore the riverfront from below the Falmouth Rapids anytime except when the river is in flood. Just plan carefully around tide and downstream current, and don't take chances. Although the Rappahannock is smaller than the Susquehanna, Potomac, and James, this is still the Bay's fourth-largest river, and it can be very powerful after heavy rains in the piedmont.

The City Dock Park is a good jumping-off point for outboard skiffs, and even a fourteen-foot tin boat with an eight- to ten-horsepower engine is capable of making the twenty-five-mile run down to Port Royal if well maintained, well equipped, and thoughtfully operated. There is no other public access, no marinas, and few houses. This stretch of the river is narrow and deep, with sand and gravel bottom scoured by the currents. On a falling tide, you will see the remains of all sorts of wharves, evidence of Fredericksburg's maritime past. (Note the names of old landings on the river chart.) There is good white perch fishing here, especially in the spring, and good fishing in deep holes for big blue catfish and channel catfish, especially at night in warm weather.

Halfway down to Port Royal, the river starts to go through deep meanders, with marshy sloughs in the side creeks and Miocene deposits of snail and oyster shells in the high banks. Look for eagles, herons, waterfowl, and shorebirds according to the season. Just above Port Royal, Cleve Marsh (Goat Island) is worth exploring if the tide will let you in.

Port Royal is an old river port, established early, along with Fredericksburg and two others, Tappahannock and Urbanna (see below), to serve colonial shipping. There is an unpaved landing here for cartop boats and light (under 300 pounds) trailered skiffs. The strip along U.S. Rt. 301 in Port Royal is unimpressive, but the back streets are full of old houses, and there is an old Episcopal church. The house on the road to the landing (now private) was a tavern, and the landing served steamboats up until the 1920s. Watch out for the old wharf pilings just upriver of the present landing. Be careful not to run into them with your boat, but by all means fish them. Some years ago, a friend of mine took three 7-pound bass on successive casts to them. (The bass fishery on this river is not as good as it is on the Potomac, but there are nice fish here for those who work it carefully.)

Below Port Royal, the river widens out, but it is still tidal fresh to Leedstown. There is no public access, although there is a commercial ramp at a campground at Leedstown, and broad expanses of open water favor larger boats. It is a good area for birds, especially geese in season at the Land's End Wildlife Management Area (Virginia Department of Game and Inland Fisheries) on the east side of Nanzatico Bay, and eagles around Horsehead Point. Commercial fishermen work catfish, perch, and rockfish (when legal), plus shad and herring in season.

Leedstown is an old river port where in 1768 a group of angry planters wrote a precursor to the Declaration of Independence called the Leedstown Resolutions. The town was active up until the end of steamboat days, but then it languished. Today, however, there is a new wharf there for a tourboat that comes up from Tappahannock to visit the nearby Ingleside Winery. On the opposite side just above Leedstown is Saunders Wharf, a restored steamboat wharf that is also a stop on the tourboat's itinerary.

This is an area of beautiful creeks, with long watersheds draining timberlands and farmlands that have often been held by the same family for generations. Timbering and farming are intense (these are shrewd business people), but they generally do a good job in both endeavors and the creeks testify to this stewardship. They are deep. Check the depths with a depth-sounder or lead line, and you'll be surprised. Occupacia, for example, has one hole that is twenty-seven feet deep and several that are twenty feet. They have big tidal fresh marshes (shading to brackish toward the mouths) mixed in with steep banks of mature hardwoods, with deep wooded swamps at the heads. This group of creeks includes Occupacia, Cat Point, Mount Landing, Hoskins, Piscataway, and Totuskey. Hoskins, at Tappahannock, has a public landing (804-367-1000), as does Totuskey, which will be described below. Hoskins suffers some from its proximity to Tappahannock, but it is still interesting. There is a campground at Naylor, at the mouth of Cat Point Creek, which may offer a launch site. Otherwise, none of the creeks has public access. If you look around carefully, you may be able to find canoe/kayak access.

On these creeks, look for all sorts of water birds, plus eagles and even, rarely, a golden eagle. You may well also find otters, beavers, muskrats, raccoons, snapping turtles, painted turtles, water snakes, bass, crappie, sunfish, white perch, yellow perch, channel catfish, gars (big ones—watch them roll to gulp air in warm weather in the deep meander turns), and herring (in April and May). These waterways fairly burst with life.

Below Totuskey, the creeks are shorter and more brackish, often full of workboats for active watermen's communities that pot for crabs and eels, tong for oysters, set pound nets and gill nets for food fish, and purse seine menhaden for crab bait. The county ramp at Simonson's Landing provides access to Lancaster Creek and the villages of Simonson and Morattico. Both are full of workboats and, in season, soft crab float operations. They are well worth a visit, and Morattico Bar, just outside the creek mouth, has been a prime fishing area for years.

Across the river, Saluda Landing (804-367-1000) provides small boat access to the head of Urbanna Creek, a nice brackish waterway with a very interesting town of the same name just below. It is well worth a visit. Check the cruise guides for information. Just below the Rt. 3 bridge near the mouth of the river at Greys Point, Upper Mill Creek Landing (804-367-1000) provides access to that creek and Locklies Creek, both behind Parrot Island. This is a nice area to explore in canoes and kayaks as well as skiffs, but be careful of exposed open water and of workboat traffic. Locklies Creek, in addition, has a large charter boat fleet.

On the north side of the river, the Corrotoman River and Carter Creek are well worth exploring if you can find access, but there are no public launch points. See the cruise guides for further information. Both waterways are written up extensively in them.

Trip Description: Totuskey Creek

Type of Waterway—Tidal fresh upstream, brackish downstream

Access and directions—Put over at the launch ramp by the Rt. 3 bridge, two miles east of Warsaw.

Trip Routes—Explore both upstream and down, then return to the bridge. Choose your route according to the tide.

Comments—Totuksey Creek is deceptive. It looks narrow and short, but you will find if you go downstream that it is nearly four miles to the mouth, and the channel is buoyed for grain boats that still come up the creek to load. They represent the last remnants of shipping for the market town of Warsaw. Above the bridge, the creek extends deep into the center of the Northern Neck, reaching north and east past Warsaw and Oldhams to butt up against the head of the Nomini Creek watershed (which drains to the Potomac). You won't be able to get that far upstream, but you will find several miles of interesting waterway with deep meanders, tidal fresh marshes, wooded banks, water birds, and mammals. Fish the holes for white perch and catfish, and in season, work the lower reaches for rockfish. Like the other large Rappahannock River creeks, there is more here than a paddler can see in a day and plenty to keep an explorer in a skiff happy.

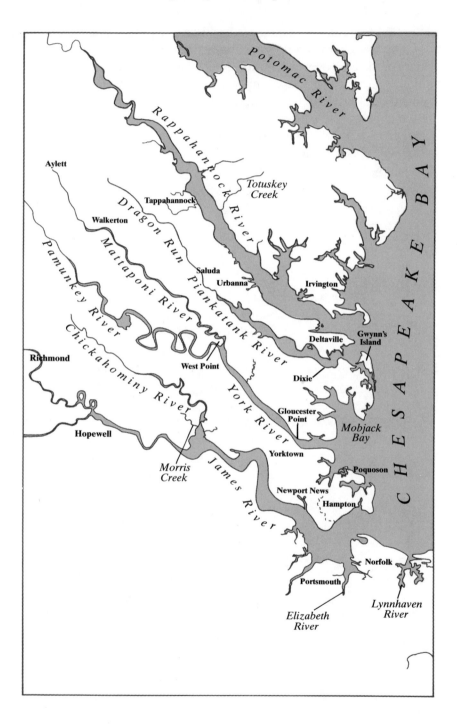

Potomac River

Rappahannock River

Aylett

Totuskey
Creek

Tappahannock

Dragon Run

Walkerton

Mattaponi River

Pamunkey River

Saluda

Piankatank River

Urbanna

Irvington

C H E S A P E A K E   B A Y

Deltaville

Gwynn's
Island

Richmond

Chickahominy River

West Point

Dixie

York River

Gloucester
Point

Mobjack
Bay

Hopewell

Morris
Creek

Yorktown

James River

Poquoson

Newport News

Hampton

Norfolk

Portsmouth

Lynnhaven
River

Elizabeth
River

eleven

Lower Western Shore

PIANKATANK RIVER, MOBJACK BAY, YORK, MATTAPONI, PAMUNKEY, POQUOSON, AND BACK RIVERS

Between the Rappahannock and the James River watersheds lies a vast chunk of Virginia's coastal plain and a small portion of its piedmont. This land drains into a large complex of rivers and creeks with great variety, including cypress swamps, tidal fresh rivers, brackish rivers, and broad salt marshes. Settlement patterns range from deep country to the edge of a major metropolitan area. The area is generally not well known, but there is plenty of access, and there are lots of places to explore.

The Piankatank is a long, narrow river corridor beginning around Millers Tavern, just south and east of Tappahannock, and flowing parallel to the Rappahannock all the way down to its mouth on the other side of Deltaville. The upper end of this waterway is the still-wild Dragon Swamp, with Dragon Run flowing down the middle of it. Halfway down, the Dragon goes through a beautiful tidal fresh delta marsh into the tidal Piankatank and becomes brackish.

It is possible to use road crossings over the Dragon to put in and take out in order to paddle the upper part of the run, but be aware that there are few places to get out of the swamp and lots of downed trees full of poison ivy vines lying across the run. Still, the area can be beautiful.

Below Rt. 17 (just south of Saluda), the Dragon is relatively clear and winding, with high banks, cypresses, and wet-ground hardwoods. It is beautiful in virtually any season. Fishing in the holes on the outsides of the turns can be good, especially for perch and sometimes for rockfish and catfish. The delta marsh is especially beautiful in August, with all of the usual tidal fresh marsh flowers plus lots of cardinal flower and the largest concentration I'm aware of on the Bay of Turk's-cap lily.

For this trip, put overboard at the Rt. 17 crossing and take out at Deep Point Landing (804-367-1000), an old lumber wharf. The distance is seven to eight miles, so plan accordingly. With a strong southerly wind, paddling in the lower river can be difficult. If it is and you decide not to go all the way to Deep Point, explore the Dragon and then paddle back to Rt. 17. Paddling against the current in the Dragon can be easier than bucking a fifteen-knot wind below.

The lower river is wide enough to require care in fourteen- to sixteen-foot skiffs, but they can be useful there, and sixteen- to twenty-foot skiffs can be excellent. Check Deep Point Landing before committing yourself to putting a big skiff overboard there. It should be fine for boats up to sixteen feet. Cartop boats also can be launched at Stampers Wharf in the bay behind Berkley Island, just up the river from the Rt. 33 bridge at Dixie. The little commercial marina at Dixie, by the old steamboat wharf, may also have a ramp.

The best feature in this part of the river is Berkley Island. It belongs to the Virginia Baptist General Board and is used as part of a summer camp. The board allows visitors but requests that they leave it as they find it. If you have any questions about using the island, call the board office in Richmond (804-672-2100). I have spent a couple of weekends there (with permission from the board) on Chesapeake Bay Foundation trips. The first weekend, a group of us foraged our meals with Euell Gibbons, the author of *Stalking the Wild Asparagus* and *Stalking the Blue-Eyed Scallop*. From April to October, you will find plenty to eat, and the island is a beautiful place.

The lower river has several nice brackish creeks to explore. Of these, Wilton, just below the bridge, is my favorite. It is narrow but deep, with high banks. Look for Miocene outcrops of coral, scallops, and oysters in the banks.

The mouth of the Piankatank is formed on the north side by Stingray Point at Deltaville and on the south side by Gwynn's Island. Milford Haven, the thoroughfare behind Gwynn's Island, is a great place to explore in small boats. Use the public ramp by the bridge at the western end of the island (804-367-1000) for paddle/oar craft and for skiffs. It is about two and one-half miles to the islands at the Hole in the Wall, the narrow eastern channel from Milford Haven to the Bay. Be careful about workboats, Coast Guard vessels (from the Milford Haven station), and pleasure boat traffic, as well as wind and afternoon thunderstorms. Nonetheless, if the weather is fine, Milford Haven is a great place to explore, with lots of coves, fishhouses, and boatyards. Gwynn's Island has a strong maritime heritage, with many natives serving as masters of ships in the merchant marine.

The islands around the Hole in the Wall are little barrier islands, with interesting dunes and marsh pools. There is good fishing just outside, along the channel edge, for croaker, spot, flounder, and trout. Some years ago, a friend from Richmond caught what is now the ten-pound-test line class world record for channel bass (sixty-nine pounds, fifteen ounces) while bottom fishing there. Once on a CBF field trip for a local high school, students and I caught a large number of juvenile channel bass in a minnow seine on the flats just behind the Hole in the Wall. Be careful of strong winds and currents in the passes around the islands, but do paddle them. This is a very good area.

Below Milford Haven, the land is sparsely settled, lying farther by road from population centers than Deltaville to the north, or Gloucester to the south. It is made up mostly of watermen's communities on the Bay shore and the East River of Mobjack Bay, plus the town of Mathews. A landing at Winter Harbor provides a launch point for cartop boats to explore the marshes and coves around the harbor. There is a small marina with a ramp nearby. You may be able to find cartop boat access around the fishhouses on Horn Harbor just below, but be respectful of the watermen's needs and of their workboat traffic.

I have had little experience with Mobjack Bay, but it is a beautiful area and well covered in cruise guides, especially for the East River, the North River, the Ware River, and the Severn River. The following are some notes on using small boats there. Town Point Landing (804-367-1000) on the East River tributary of Put In Creek provides access to the head of the creek (at the town of Mathews) and to the East River, with nice tidal fresh marshes at the head, although you may need your push-pole up there. There is no public access on the North River, but it is pretty and sparsely settled. Warehouse Landing on the Ware River (804-367-1000) has a ramp for access. The Ware is more heavily settled, but it also is beautiful. The south side of Severn River is Guinea Neck, a longtime center for commercial fishing. Some of the most skillful watermen in the Bay hail from here.

The mouth of the York is big-boat water, well covered in the cruise guides. You may want to stop in at the visitor center of the Virginia Institute of Marine Science, one of the Bay's major research labs (call 804-684-7000 for information), and at the Yorktown Victory Center across the river (757-887-1776).

The York is about thirty-five miles long, straight and wide, with a number of military facilities. The land on both sides of the lower end is growing fast, developing suburbs to the Williamsburg/Newport News/Hampton metropolitan area. Major sources of jobs include the Newport News Shipbuilding and Dry Dock Co. (now a division of Tenneco, Inc., and one of the largest shipyards in the country) and the Langley NASA Center.

The upper river is less developed. On the south side, the York River State Park (757-566-3036) is well worth a visit. Explore its marshes on foot by its walking trails. It is an excellent facility. On the other side, the Poropotank River is a large creek with brackish marshes below and tidal fresh marshes above. Small boats can launch at Tanyard Landing (804-367-1000).

The York River splits at the town of West Point into the Mattaponi and Pamunkey rivers. These two rivers reach up into the piedmont north and west of Richmond. Both of the Pamunkey's major tributaries, the North and South Anna rivers, have significant rapids at and just above the fall line. You will find write-ups on them in the Virginia white water guidebooks (check a canoe/kayak store). The Mattaponi's tributary Matta, Po, and Ni rivers are smaller and do not go back far enough to develop significant white water.

Just below the fall line, the Mattaponi and the Pamunkey drain extensive hardwood swamps and vast commercial timberlands. They are not large enough to be navigable for shipping from the fall line, and their strong tides and narrow channels surely made them difficult to navigate in seventeenth- and eighteenth-century sailing vessels, which may have deterred shipping. Thus no major ports like Fredericksburg or Richmond grew up on them. For such shipping as there was, small landings grew up over the years at a number of places whose names reflect that use.

Instead, West Point was the major port, and the two rivers were left to the remaining Indian tribes of the same names and to a few other people who chose to farm, timber, fish, hunt, and trap. Today, the Mattaponi and the Pamunkey are largely passed over by people seeking broader open water, beaches, and deep-water slips for cruising boats, but they hold some of the finest natural areas in Virginia. It is no accident that The Nature Conservancy has made the wooded swamp bottomlands of the Pamunkey a priority area. Both rivers are jewels for small boat explorers, who will find them unspoiled and interesting.

The Mattaponi is tidal fresh for nearly its whole length, growing brackish only down between Melrose Landing (804-367-1000) and Waterfence Landing. Both offer launch ramps, as does the landing at West Point (804-367-1000). The characteristic meander pattern of the river produces broad marshes and deep water in the turns. Upriver, there are some fine old houses scattered on what fastland there is between the marshes and the swamps. The river is good for skiffs and paddle/oar craft, but be careful of very strong tides. See below for a description of the river between Walkerton and Aylett and a note about the tides.

The Mattaponi is an important river for spawning rockfish, shad, and herring. The former Virginia State rockfish record, sixty-one pounds, was caught on bait by a bank fisherman on the lower river, but the runs of shad and herring have declined. The Mattaponi and Pamunkey Indians still fish drift nets for shad, but as of this writing, the shad runs are a cause for major concern.

The Pamunkey is the larger river, deep and strong. It too offers huge marshes and an Indian reservation. There is one large old town site at Cumberland Landing. This is one of those places that was once prosperous but lost out by a vote or two in balloting to choose the state capital. The Cumberland peninsula had had all its timber cut over by the 1860s, and landowners tried to build rice paddies along Holts Creek, on the upriver side, but failed. That failure is ironic, because most of the marshes in Holts Creek are wild rice. In the Civil War, General McClellan camped his army there briefly during the Peninsula Campaign of 1862. Old photographs taken then show just how denuded the land was. Since then, strong second growth has developed there, and the peninsula is now deeply wooded. It is presently the site of a private hospital.

The rest of the river shore is largely farms and timberland. The Indians fish it commercially for catfish and perch, as do a few other watermen. If you look, you will find eagles, ospreys, waterfowl, otters, muskrats, bass, pickerel, white perch, yellow perch, catfish, and rockfish. The landing at Lester Manor (804-367-1000) is a good central location for local exploration by paddle/oar craft and wider exploration by skiff. One good trip by outboard is from Lester Manor to Aylett on the

Mattaponi or vice versa. Plan for the tides carefully. Be aware that there aren't any facilities except at West Point, and the only public landings are those listed above. The Mattaponi and the Pamunkey provide one of the most overlooked areas on the whole Bay system for small boat exploring.

It is a big switch from the Mattaponi/Pamunkey complex to the Bay shore below the York River. Here are high-salinity salt marshes, mostly along the shore and in the creeks and coves. This is mostly big boat water, again covered in the cruise guides, but with two exceptions. The first is the Big Salt Marsh at Poquoson, the largest marsh on the western shore of the Chesapeake (see description below). The other is the Grandview Natural Preserve, owned by the City of Hampton (804-727-6347). It is the long, thin, elbow-shaped point that forms the south side of the mouth of Back River.

Grandview is closed to automobile traffic, leaving its beach, marshes, and dunes for us to explore on foot or by canoe/kayak. If you are paddling, launch your boat at Grundland Creek Park (804-727-6347) and explore the back waters of the preserve. Then walk the beach for a complete look at this interesting area. Be careful, though, in spring, of nesting willets, oystercatchers, and the endangered least tern. If you are in a skiff, launch at Dandy Point Ramp (804-367-1000), but beware: the channels are narrow, surrounded by shallow flats. Those flats, however, have interesting grass beds to go along with the marshes. There is a good drop-off with a strong tide rip at the point, forming an excellent bottom fishing area for spot, croaker, and trout. Just outside the mouth, in fifteen to twenty feet of water, is a lumpy shell bottom called Bluefish Rock, a good area for blues and cobia. All told, Grandview is an excellent natural area within the Hampton Roads metropolitan region.

Trip Description: Mattaponi River, Aylett to Walkerton

Type of Waterway—Tidal fresh

Directions and Access—Use the public ramp at Aylett (804-367-1000), beside the Rt. 360 bridge at the upper end. Below, use the ramp at Walkerton (it's privately owned, but a modest donation to the local rescue squad will get you overboard), on the downriver side of Rt. 629. To reach Walkerton from Aylett, go west on Rt. 360 to Central Garage, then left (east) on Rt. 30 six miles to a left turn onto Rt. 629. Follow Rt. 629 to the bridge and cross the river to Walkerton.

Trip Route—The trip is about nine miles. In any boat, choose your route by the tide. You'll see why in a minute. Check the tide tables and go with the flow, from Aylett to Walkerton or vice versa as appropriate.

Cautions—Be well prepared. There are no services and few takeouts. Don't fight the tide; let it work for you.

Comments—The village of Walkerton, seventy miles above the mouth of the York and surrounded by tidal fresh marshes, has the distinction of the highest average vertical tide range in the whole Bay system: 3.9 feet. (You can look it up in the NOAA *Tide Tables*.) Wave resonance and basin geometry work together to produce the effect. The tides can be five feet with the moon, wind, and barometer driving them. They are also asymmetrical. The Mattaponi ebbs for seven hours and floods for five and one-half. The current does not necessarily reverse at the times of maximum or minimum water levels, but use them as guides when planning a trip.

This portion of the Mattaponi is moderately deep, with wooded swamp along the bank. It is a traditional shad and herring area in the spring, though fishermen have had to work hard for them in recent years. There are also white and yellow perch, catfish, rockfish in season, bass, crappie, and pickerel. The banks are high, with some creek marshes in the first couple of miles. Below Roanes Wharf, the river widens out, with large yellow pond lily marshes, some rice, and other tidal fresh plants. Little slough channels often cut back behind the lily pad beds along the shore.

At the foot of this stretch is a very old house, Whitehall, the home of a summer camp where I spent three seasons as a counselor. You will see the green cabins along the river shore just below the house. The schedule at the camp is built around the tide, changing every two weeks to adjust to it. One of the favorite activities at low tide is to play hide-and-seek by canoe in the marsh guts just below the camp, inside the turn before Walkerton. The outside of that turn we call "Gar Playground," as the big prehistoric fish roll to gulp air on summer days. The Mattaponi is a beautiful, unspoiled river.

Trip Description: Big Salt Marsh, Poquoson

Type of Waterway—Salt marsh

Directions and Access—Commercial marina ramp at Poquoson Marina, on Rens Road in Poquoson.

Trip Route—Around Cow Island, seven miles, or explore Lloyds Bay, two to five miles.

Cautions—High winds over the marsh can make paddling difficult. Also, powerboat traffic requires caution, especially in the Bennett Creek channel.

Comments—"Come run a canoe trip for our girl scout troop," invited a friend twenty-five years ago. "Is there any marsh at Poquoson?" I asked. She chuckled. I was new to Poquoson then. Her husband took me out into the middle of Lloyd's Bay in a skiff. He shut the engine down and we drifted, completely surrounded by cordgrass. True to its name, this is the biggest salt marsh on the western shore.

The Big Marsh is built on a large, firm deposit of coarse coastal plain sand stretching from the mouth of the Poquoson River down to the mouth of Back River. Native Americans fished and oystered here, and Europeans settled the area in the seventeenth century, farming the fastland, grazing livestock on the marsh, and harvesting seafood. Islands in the Big Marsh bear names like Cow and Goat, and the whole area has come to be known collectively as Bull Island. Calling a person a Bull Islander was once cause for a fight, but now residents carry the name with pride. Cattle roamed the marshes freely in summer in the early days. There is an old joke that Poquoson experienced a cultural revolution in the early nineteenth century when people started fencing cattle in instead of out.

Farming in the area gradually declined as the land became more and more settled. Industry came to the peninsula, especially in the form of Newport News Shipbuilding and Dry Dock Co. and the U.S. Government. Highways grew apace. Today Poquoson is proud to be an incorporated city, though it is mostly a suburban community feeding the Langley NASA Center that adjoins the lower end of the marsh and the Newport News shipyard. The area is not as built up as, say, Annapolis or the Norfolk-Portsmouth complex, but the Big Marsh is still a pocket of country in a residential area. Standing on a salt meadow at the edge of Sandy Bay, one finds a vista of broad marshes and tidal guts broken only by the outline of the Lunar Lander at Langley.

Maybe it is no longer wilderness, but the Big Marsh is still a prime natural area. It is, in fact, part of the Plum Tree Island National Wildlife Refuge, managed by the U.S. Fish and Wildlife Service. The best area for exploration by small boat is the guts off Lloyds Bay. The circular route around Cow Island, up through Sandy Bay, and back around to Bennett Creek is a particularly good day trip in a canoe, though the last couple of miles back into Bennett Creek against a summertime southerly breeze can make a long afternoon.

This marsh is a classic. It is full of birds, especially ospreys, gulls, terns, herons, and egrets. In May, June, and July, some shorebirds are around, and fall brings waterfowl. There are otters, muskrats, and fat raccoons. The waters abound with young menhaden and spot, killifish, silversides, mullet, grass shrimp, and crabs. The deep hole in Lloyds Bay is rimmed with oyster bars. A bottom rig baited with peeler crabs or grass shrimp will sometimes turn up pan-sized trout, croakers, and spot. Large bluefish occasionally forage silversides in the eelgrass beds on the north shore of Cow Island, where it fronts on the Poquoson River. The shallow flats hold hard clams for those with rakes.

Access to the Big Marsh is easily achieved. Within the Poquoson Marina complex on Rens Road, there are two launch ramps. The one beside the bait shop belongs to the marina. It is well kept, and there is a fee for using it, but the user has rights to restrooms, washdown hoses, and fish cleaning tables. A hundred yards to the right, there is another ramp that is free to the public. It is not particularly well kept and has no facilities. This ramp is adequate for canoes and skiffs, though users should bear in mind that it is slick and the dropoff at the end of it is steep.

Poquoson Marina's growth over the past twenty years is an index of the changes that have taken place on the peninsula. In 1970, William Carmines was building his classic diamond-stern workboats a quarter-mile back up Rens Road, and the Dryden family was operating a fishhouse next to the public ramp. Most of the watermen who tied up there were hauling seines on the Poquoson Flats at the mouth of the river, setting pound nets along the Bay shore, or patent tonging for hard clams. The marina had a few slips, a tiny bait shack, and a small new restaurant.

Mr. Carmines has retired now. The elder Drydens have died, and the fishhouse is all but closed. But there are four times as many slips, for both power- and sailboats, and people from as far away as Norfolk rent them. Fishermen with boats on trailers line up at the launch ramps on weekends. The bait shop sells tackle and books several charter boats. The Virginia Marine Resources Commission has set up a field office next to the bait shop, operating two patrol boats out of the marina. The restaurant is large and busy.

The marina is a beehive of activity, but it is not an unpleasant jumping-off point, and the restaurant can provide a good breakfast before you set out or a welcome seafood dinner on your return. There is one caution, though. Boat traffic, from both pleasure boats and workboats, can be heavy. Small boats do well to stay to the channel edges and to be cautious crossing Bennett Creek. This is no place to be careless.

It is important to watch the weather when exploring the Big Marsh. The area is exposed, and winds over twelve knots can make life unpleasant for canoes and kayaks. The lower end of the marsh used to be a bombing range for Langley Air Force Base, and there are unexploded shells there, so it is absolutely off-limits to the public.

In spite of cautions about boat traffic and winds, the Big Marsh remains a prime area for exploration in small boats. It is a classic salt marsh of great peace and beauty on the edge of a large metropolitan area.

twelve

The James River and Hampton Roads

The James is the other major river in the Chesapeake system, about seven-tenths the size of the Potomac, or about twice as large as the Rappahannock. It begins on the Allegheny plateau in Highland County as the Cowpasture River, at the West Virginia border, with a major tributary, the Jackson River, coming in from farther west at Covington. It runs a long course through the piedmont and reaches the fall line at Richmond, which is, of course, the port city that grew up at its head of navigation. The tidal James flows about ninety miles from Richmond down to its mouth at Hampton Roads.

The James is the cradle of European settlement in the New World, with exploration into the river and settlement of the Jamestown Colony occurring in 1607. Other towns followed quickly, including Hampton in 1610 (the oldest continuous settlement in the New World) and Bermuda Hundred, about sixty-five miles above the mouth, in 1613. Like the Potomac, the James is a wide river, well suited to early navigation and hence valuable for opening up both the extensive country along its banks and the fertile piedmont lands above Richmond.

There is an old saying that we can't look ahead more than three generations or back more than three generations except with great effort. It is a difficult but interesting exercise to try to think what the James was like in the early seventeenth century, with a Virginia colony struggling to survive while its members tried to find an economic base to sustain it. Within ten years after settlement, the colonists were successfully farming, cutting timber from virgin forests, and even sawing the wood with a primitive sawmill on the lower James.

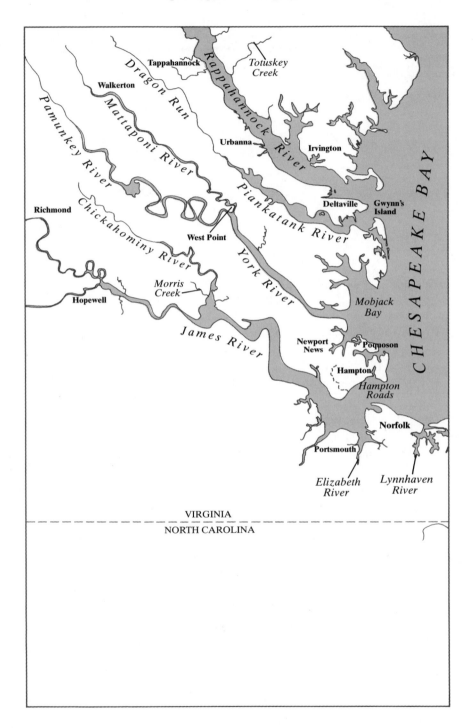

As the seventeenth century drew on, tobacco and timber developed a solid base for the colony, and the James River grew into an essential resource, both for natural harbors like Hampton Roads for shipping, and for food. Though the James never reached the prominence of the Potomac as a fishing river, it has always had the same combination of shad, herring, sturgeon, and rockfish. The extensive shoals at its mouth and just above have always produced tremendous numbers of oysters. Indeed, it is the Bay's major producer of seed oysters. The marshes along the river and its tributaries provide good habitat for waterfowl, eagles, ospreys, herons, and other water birds.

With all these riches, the river above Jamestown also developed an extensive plantation society similar to the one on the Northern Neck. Several great estates have been restored and are open to the public, like Shirley, which has been owned by the same family (the Carters) since early in the seventeenth century. Others include Berkeley, Westover, and Riverview, the latter two having the benefit of the beautiful and long Herring Creek, which is reminiscent of the Rappahannock's Occupacia and Totuskey.

The James has had its problems, especially in this century. Richmond has a long history of sewage problems, especially combined sewer overflows from the old part of the city (where the storm drains are linked with the sanitary sewers). Plenty of red clay soil from the James's wide piedmont watershed has come downriver and settled. The chemical industry in Hopewell has had problems, especially the debacle with the insecticide Kepone in the early 1970s that resulted first in a full and then a partial closure of the river's fisheries that lasted until 1988. Down at the mouth, at Hampton Roads, there are serious toxic problems on the Southern Branch of the Elizabeth River.

Today, however, the Clean Water Act has had an effect on Richmond sewage and Hopewell toxics. A testimony to the improvement is the fact that the prestigious BASS Masters Classic fishing tournament was held here in 1988, '89, and '90, using virtually the whole river from Richmond down to and including the whole of its biggest tributaries, the Appomattox and the Chickahominy. There are still problems with combined sewer overflows, though Richmond is struggling to deal with them. Nonpoint source problems, for instance sediment and agricultural nutrients, and toxics on the Elizabeth River are also concerns. Like the Potomac, no river system with a couple of million people around it is ever safe. Despite the problems, though, there is a lot to enjoy.

The river from Richmond down to Turkey Island (the Presquile National Wildlife Refuge) is a narrow, wooded, powerful waterway like the Rappahannock below Fredericksburg, only more so. The transition from free-flowing stream to tidal river at Richmond is interesting. You can walk the fall line trails of the James River Park within the city limits, take a raft trip with a commercial outfitter, or, if you are experienced in running white water, paddle with a local club like the Coastal Canoeists. The fall line has some major rapids.

Ancarrow's Landing (804-367-1000) provides access to the city dock area just below the fall line. Even though tidal, this portion of the river is very powerful, especially in flood. Hence it should be treated with great caution. Launch ramps just below Richmond include Osborne Pike and Deep Bottom on the north bank and Dutch Gap on the south (call 804-367-1000 for information on all three). They provide access where the river is still narrow but with lots of sloughs and cuts, many of them old gravel pits. Fishing in this section for bass, crappie, and catfish can be excellent.

Just below Deep Bottom are Curles Neck, a private and very well-managed marsh, and the Presquile refuge, a complex that draws large numbers of waterfowl each winter. Presquile is open to the public on a limited basis (call 804-733-8042 or 530-1397 for information). Turkey Island, which was initially a meander before the Corps of Engineers cut a channel at its base in the 1930s, has a good combination of agricultural fields, two large marshes (on the east side and the north end), and a deep wooded swamp laced by two creeks. Look especially for owls and wood ducks in the swamp creeks. The mainland end of the cable ferry that serves the island is the site of the seventeenth-century town of Bermuda Hundred, built at a point where the river narrows down, a natural site for a colonial port. Canoes and kayaks should exercise *great* caution about powerful currents in these narrow channels and about powerboats, especially high-speed bass boats and tugs pushing gravel barges. The same cautions would apply for outboard skiffs. Nonetheless, the Presquile area is a great one. The Chesapeake Bay Foundation has been running field trips here for fifteen years in all but the dead of winter. There is always a great deal to see.

Just downriver is Hopewell, formerly an old port city but now an industrial town. The Hopewell Yacht Club (804-541-3308) offers good public access for a fee to launch by the Rt. 10 bridge crossing the Appomattox River. The Appomattox is a pretty, tidal fresh river, and it offers reasonable access to Presquile for skiffs.

Below Hopewell, the river widens out to half a mile or more, with a winding channel between marsh islands and spoil banks. (There is a great deal of piedmont soil here, just as there is in the Potomac at Alexandria.) Fishing for big blue catfish and channel catfish with cut bait around the tide rips of the Benjamin Harrison Bridge at Hopewell can be great. It is well worth exploring around the marsh islands between Tar Bay and the main channel, but this is big boat water, with skiffs of sixteen feet or more strongly recommended. There is a good commercial ramp and a marina at Jordan Point, at the south end of the bridge.

The best places to explore below the bridge are side creeks, especially the large ones, which, as noted, are reminiscent of those on the Rappahannock. Herring Creek on the north side winds back past Berkeley, Westover, and Riverview plantations, with beautiful wild rice marshes, waterfowl, and plenty of fish. Powell Creek on the opposite side has a major eagle roost owned by the Virginia Chapter of The Nature Conservancy. Be careful to read posted instructions if you go into Powell. Other creeks like Wards, Kittewan, and Upper Chippokes are also beautiful and productive, with tidal fresh marshes and cypress trees, but with little public access, for which reason they are difficult to explore by paddle/oar craft.

For canoes and kayaks go to the Chickahominy, a beautiful tidal fresh river that is described in more detail below.

Below the Chickahominy, public access is still limited on both sides, but interesting places to visit on foot or by car include Jamestown National Historical Park (757-229-1607) on the north side and the Hog Island Wildlife Management Area on the south side (804-367-1000). Hog Island is an excellent area for waterfowl.

Below Jamestown, the river starts to get brackish, and below Hog Island it widens out even more. Because of the James's proximity to the mouth of the Bay, salinity increases rapidly in this section, the site of its great oyster nursery. On the north side within the city of Newport News, Denbigh Park Boat Ramp (804-367-1000) gives excellent access to the beautiful Warwick River, a fine waterway for paddle/oar craft and skiffs, with salt marsh below and brackish/tidal fresh marsh above. If you are running an outboard on the Warwick River, be careful of shoals and channels. On the south side, the Pagan River runs up to Smithfield, and its tributaries are an interesting mix of brackish and tidal fresh marshes, but there is no public access. You may be able to find a commercial launch ramp.

Just below the mouth of the Pagan River is a fine salt marsh at the Ragged Island Creek Wildlife Management Area (804-367-1000), with good trails to walk out onto the marsh and into the wooded hammocks scattered around in it. If you search, you may be able to find an access point on Ragged Island Creek to explore the back side of the marsh. This is an excellent area, much like the Big Salt Marsh at Poquoson. Just as Poquoson offers the contrast of standing in a big salt marsh and looking up at the Langley Lunar Lander, so at Ragged Island Creek, you can stand in the middle of its marsh and look across the river at the Newport News shipyard. The Bay country is often a study in contrasts.

The James now becomes increasingly urbanized, but it is worth noting that the Nansemond River has extensive brackish and tidal fresh marshes within the city of Suffolk, and almost Mattaponi-sized tides (3.8 feet). Obviously they call for the same kind of care as the Mattaponi, but the area is interesting. Bennetts Creek Park (804-367-1000) near the mouth and Constants Wharf in downtown Suffolk offer access.

Within the city of Norfolk, the Elizabeth River spreads in four directions, with much of each branch industrialized and urbanized, but with two tributaries well worth a visit: the Lafayette and the Western Branch. Both are suburban but, while not pristine, they are definitely attractive, with birds, fish, and salt marshes. In the Lafayette River, use the Haven Creek Boat Ramp by the bridge on Granby Street or Lafayette Park just upriver. On the Western Branch, use the ramp at City Park in Portsmouth (804-367-1000). Be careful about commercial and pleasure boat traffic, but fish and explore. These are two pretty rivers. Beyond Norfolk, Lynnhaven Inlet, at the mouth of the Bay, offers good salt marshes and wide shallow bays to explore in small boats, even though much of the shoreline is becoming suburbanized. Use the ramps at nearby commercial marinas, but be careful of boat traffic and strong currents in the inlet. Use the ramp at Seashore State Park (757-481-2131) for Broad Bay and Linkhorn Bay. These are much the best for paddle/oar craft.

Trip Description: Chickahominy River

Type of Waterway—Tidal fresh

Directions and Access—Morris Creek boat ramp (804-367-1000) in the Chickahominy Wildlife Management Area, just north of Rt. 5 and west of the river on Rt. 623. You may be able to find commercial access at a marina just upriver at Holdcroft and also across the river at the camp-ground on Gordon Creek. The entrance to the latter is on Rt. 5 just east of the bridge.

Trip Routes—In paddle/oar craft, explore Morris Creek. In skiffs, explore the creek and the river. See below for other possibilities.

Cautions—Strong winds and tides, especially on the main river, plus high-speed bass boat traffic.

Comments—The Chickahominy begins as a swamp north of Richmond. It flows east and then south into the James just above Jamestown. Part of it was dammed at Walkers by the city of Newport News as a water supply reservoir in 1938, forming Chickahominy Lake, which is beautiful in its own right, but the lower eighteen miles of the river are tidal and a longtime favorite of mine, with deep channel meanders between cypress swamps fronted by tidal fresh marshes. The river is full of bass and every other fish that frequents a tidal fresh river. It also has otters, eagles, muskrats, and lots of waterfowl. Fastland is limited along its banks, so there is very little settlement.

Morris Creek itself offers a variety of coves, meanders, and marshes. The seasons are distinct and well worth following here. Look for water-fowl like teal in the early fall, feeding on wild rice, and then for the beautiful heather tones of the cypresses as their needles turn colors. Winter offers more waterfowl and good fishing for chain pickerel. Spring offers a variety of flowering trees and shrubs, plus a strong run of herring, especially up at Walkers Dam, the head of navigation. Summer is lush. There is no other word for it. Fish for bass year-round, but change your techniques with the seasons.

If you can get access at the campground across the river, a nice trip by canoe or kayak with midday high tide is to paddle up Gordon Creek in the morning, through Nayses Bay at midday, and down Nettles Creek in the afternoon. A short paddle downstream on the main river will bring you back to your launch point. Gordon Island in the middle of this circuit is a well-managed hunt club. The owners have kept the area in its wild state, but they also own some of the surrounding marshes, and they post them at certain points of the gunning season, so obey signs that you see.

In a skiff, explore upriver all the way to Walkers Dam. Note that Yarmouth and Shipyard creeks meet like Gordon and Nettles to form Wright Island, also a private gunning club. Obey the signs, but look around. Note that the names suggest early settlement here. Cypress is great boat lumber, so much of the swamp was logged in the seventeenth, eighteenth, and nineteenth centuries. Most of the lumber was shipped out, but obviously some was used here to build ships. Some timber is cut today, but mostly the cypress has been allowed to grow back into mature second growth.

There is a vast complex of creeks and guts to explore in the Chickahominy. The river is well known to bass fishermen but largely unknown to the general public. It deserves to be well loved. It is a treasure.

INDEX

Index

Index

187

Index